U Visa Victim of Crime Petition

How People Without Legal Status Can Get The U Visa If They Are Victims of Crime

Attorney Brian D. Lerner

BDL
LAW OFFICES OF
BRIAN D. LERNER
A PROFESSIONAL CORPORATION

ATTORNEY DRAFTED IMMIGRATION PETITIONS

By

Brian D. Lerner

Attorney at Law

Disclaimer and Terms of Use:

Effort has been made to ensure that the information in this book is accurate and complete. However, the author and the publisher do not warrant that this particular petition will mirror or be exactly as your situation. There has not been any attorney-client agreement created by the purchase of this petition or application. No legal advice has occurred. The cases, regulations and/or statutes cited may change at any time without notice.

ISBN: 978-1-958990-14-8

INTRODUCTION

There are a multitude of different immigration petitions and applications. They are complex and full of requirements. Obviously, it would be best to hire an immigration attorney to best prepare the petitions and applications. However, this can certainly cost thousands of dollars.

The next best option is to get a sample of the petition written by an experienced immigration attorney. The samples cost a fraction what would be charged by an immigration attorney. However, while the reader has to alter, amend and change the parts of the sample petition to reflect their actual situation, it is a fantastic roadmap for them to use. If the reader has purchased the entire petition or application, they will have real live samples of cover letters, forms, declarations, affidavits and the necessary exhibits to use. The samples come from real cases and the names of those clients have been redacted to protect the privacy of that person or corporation.

These are petitions and applications that have been drafted by an experienced immigration attorney with over 25 years of experience. Get the benefits of that experience without the costs.

CONTENTS

About the Law Offices of Brian D. Lerner

The Law Offices of Brian D. Lerner, APC. The law practice consists of Immigration and Nationality Law and everything involved with and regarding immigration which includes citizenship, investment visas, family and employment visas, removal and deportation hearings, appeals, waivers, adjustment, consulate processing and all types of immigration and citizenship matters. Thousands of families have been reunited and/or permitted to stay in the U.S. and/or return to the U.S. because of the successful work of Immigration Attorney Brian D. Lerner.

This law offices handles all types of immigration cases including family based and employment based. Immigration issues range from immigration court proceedings to trying to fix what paralegals may have done that was neither correct nor proper. Foreign nationals must have experience lawyers admitted to practice law.

The Law Offices of Brian D. Lerner, APC, handles cases arising from business visas, work permits, Green Cards, non-immigrant visas, deportation, citizenship, appeals and all areas of immigration. The Law Offices of Brian D. Lerner, APC does EB-5 Investor Visas, H-1B Specialty Occupation, L-1 Intracompany Transferee, E-2 Treaty Investor, E-1 Treaty Trader, O-1 Extraordinary Ability among others. Regarding immigrant visas for the Green Card, the firm does PERM and advanced degree PERM, Family Petitions, and Extraordinary Alien Petitions. In addition to affirmative petitions, the Law Firm represents people in people in deportation and removal hearings, including political asylum, withholding of removal, and convention against torture cases.

Brian D. Lerner has been certified as an expert in Immigration & Nationality Law by the California State Bar, Board of Legal Specialization since 2000 and has been re-certified three times. He now passes on his decades of experience by allowing the Reader, Law Schools, Professors and other Immigration Attorneys to purchase sample petitions on every facet of Immigration Law.

About the U-Visa

If you have been a victim of crime and are here in the U.S. illegally, or your status will expire, then the U-1 Visa could be for you. If approved, then you could get legal status to remain here in the U.S. and then apply for residency three years later. Another benefit of the U Visa is that if you are inadmissible on other grounds, the U-1 regulations would permit you to apply for waivers of those grounds of inadmissibility, even if you would not otherwise qualify for a particular waiver.

Finally, the derivative benefits for a U-1 Visa are excellent. This means that if you have spouse and/or unmarried children and even other relatives, they may be able to get derivative U-1 Visas based on yours. Thus, this book will allow you to see a guide of how it is done, prepared and submitted.

ATTORNEY COVER LETTER

Law Offices of Brian D. Lerner

A PROFESSIONAL CORPORATION

CERTIFIED SPECIALIST IN IMMIGRATION AND NATIONALITY LAW
ADMITTED TO THE U.S. SUPREME COURT

LONG BEACH, CALIFORNIA
(562) 495-0554

CARSON, CALIFORNIA
(310) 684-5400

July 11, 2018

USCIS - Vermont Service Center
75 Lower Welden Street
St. Albans, VT 05479

RE: Application for U Visa and Waiver of Inadmissibility
Applicant: [redacted]

Dear Officer:

Mr. [redacted] (hereinafter "Applicant") has retained our office to represent him in his immigration matters. Specifically, we have been retained to prepare a U visa on his behalf pursuant to section 101(a)(15)(U) of the Immigration and Nationality Act (hereafter "INA" or "Act"), 8 U.S.C. § 1101(a)(15)(U), based on the fact that (1) Applicant was victim of **Assault/Battery, Robbery, and Willful Cruelty to a Child**, as the Applicant's daughter, [redacted] also suffered an injury during the incident, (2) he possesses information regarding this crime, and (3) he was helpful in the investigation of this crime. Applicant is a person of good moral character who would suffer hardship if he was forced to remain outside the United States. Granting Applicant a waiver necessary for the U visa is in the public interest generally because local law enforcement use of U visas sends a crucial message to immigrants that they can report crime and to perpetrators that they cannot victimize immigrants with impunity. A waiver in this case furthers that public benefit and American humanitarian values because Applicant assisted, and continues to assist, local authorities in the persecution of the perpetrator of this crime.

Enclosed you will find the documents to establish eligibility for a U visa.[1]

FORMS

Forms:	**Description:**
G-1145	E-Notification of Application/Petition Acceptance;
G-28	Notice of Entry of Appearance as Attorney or Accredited Representative;
I-192	Application for Advance Permission to Enter as a Nonimmigrant along with Filing Fee of $930.00;

[1] On September 5, 2007, Department of Homeland Security issued regulations that establish the process for U Visas. See New Classification for Victims of Criminal Activity; Eligibility for "U" Nonimmigrant Status, 72 Fed. Reg. 53014 (interim rule with request for comments Sept. 17, 2007)(to be codified at 8 C.F.R. pts 103, 212, 214, 248, 274a and 299)(hereinafter Interim Rule).

I-765	Application for Employment Authorization;
I-918	Petition for a U Nonimmigrant Status; and
I-918B	U Nonimmigrant Status Certification.

Enclosed are copies of two Immigration Photographs of Applicant.

EXHIBITS

Exhibits **Description:**

Documents showing psychological condition of Applicant.

1. Declaration of Applicant about Physical and Mental Assault of the Criminal Activity perpetrated against he and his Family;
2. Psychological Evaluation of the Applicant;

Identification Documents

3. Passport of the Applicant;
4. Voter's Registration Card, and Mexican Consular Identification Card of the Applicant;
5. Copy of the Applicant's Birth Certificate with English Translation;
6. Copy of the Birth Certificates of the Applicant's Spouse and Children;
7. Copy of the the Marriage Certificate of the Applicant and the Applicant's Spouse;

Criminal and Immigration Related Documents

8. Copy of the Police Incident Report of the Applicant;
9. Letter from Lt. Robert ROSIN of the Oakland Police Department to the Applicant's Spouse concerning the Investigation of the Applicant's ongoing case;
10. Court Documents of the Applicant from October 21, 2010;
11. Removal Order of the Applicant from July of 2011;

Letters of Support from Friends and Family of the Applicant

12. Letters of Support from Friends and Family of the Applicant;
13. Photographs of the Applicant and his family;

Exhibits Regarding Conditions in Mexico

14. World Report 2017: Mexico-Human Rights Watch;
15. Amnesty International – Mexico Annual Report 2017-2018;
16. U.S. Department of State – Mexico Travel Advisory 2018;
17. U.S. Department of State – Mexico: Secretary for Civilian Security, Democracy, and Human Rights;
18. Mexico 2018 Crime & Safety Report: Mexico City - OSAC; and
19. **'The Borgen Project,'** The Blog, Top Diseases in Mexico, Symptoms, Prevalence & Treatment, October 2016.

I. INTRODUCTION

Pursuant to INA § 101 (a)(15)(U), 8 U.S.C. § 1101 (a)(15)(U), the Attorney General may grant non-immigrant alien status (U-visa) when:

I. the alien has **suffered substantial physical or mental abuse** as a result of having been a victim of **criminal activity** described in the clause (iii)

II. the alien (or in the case of an alien child under the age of 16, the parent, guardian, or next friend of the alien) **possesses information** concerning criminal activity described in the clause (iii);

III. the alien (or in the case of an alien child under the age of 16, the parent, guardian, or next friend of the alien) **has been helpful**, is being helpful, or is likely to be helpful to a Federal, State, or local law enforcement official, to a Federal, State, or local prosecutor, to a Federal or State judge, to the Service, or to other Federal, State, or local authorities investigating or **prosecuting criminal activity** described in the clause (iii); and

IV. the criminal activity described in the clause (iii) **violated the laws of the United States** or occurred in the United States (including in Indian country and military installations) or the territories and possessions of the United States.

We are submitting documents, psychological reports, and other evidence included with this package to demonstrate that the applicant is a person who suffered direct and proximate harm as a result of the commission of one of the enumerated felonies, suffered substantial mental abuse, possesses information about the crime, and helped with the investigation of the perpetrator.

II.
THE CRIME COMMITTED IS OF A TYPE OF CRIMINAL ACTIVITY LISTED IN INA§ 101(a)(15)(U)(iii)

Pursuant to Code §101(a)(15)(U)(iii) of the Immigration and Nationality Act, obstruction of justice is one of the underlying criminal activities that qualifies the victim for a nonimmigrant alien status (U-visa).[2] Applicant is a direct victim of the justice system as the listed crime of Felonious Assault Threats under California Penal Code Section 245.

Qualifying Criminal Activity includes one or more of the following or any similar activities in violation of federal, state, or local criminal laws: abduction; aggravated assault; blackmail; domestic violence; extortion; false imprisonment; **attempted robbery; felonious assault**; female genital mutilation; fraud in foreign labor contracting, hostage (being held as a); incest; involuntary servitude; kidnapping; manslaughter; murder; obstruction of justice; peonage; perjury; prostitution; rape; sexual assault; sexual contact (abusive); sexual exploitation; slave trade; criminal threats, torture; trafficking; unlawful criminal restraint;_witness tampering; or attempt, **willful cruelty to a child;** conspiracy, or solicitation to commit any of these crimes. INA §101(a)(15)(U)(iii); Any "similar activity" refers to criminal offenses in which "the nature and elements of the offenses are substantially similar to the statutorily enumerated list of criminal activities." 8 C.F.R. §214.14(a)(9); 72 FR 53014, 53018 (Sept. 17, 2007).

On January 27, 2018, the Applicant, his spouse, and his children went to visit the Applicant's cousin, █████ and her family in Oakland, CA. The Applicant's family spent the whole day at his cousin's house. The Applicant and his spouse left the house about 10:15 p.m. when they realized that they had forgotten the baby's bottle. The Applicant and his family drove back to his cousin's house to retrieve the baby's bottle.

They noticed a honda accord parked on the curb that was not there when they left. While the Applicant and his spouse while carrying their baby in her arms, walked toward his cousin's house on the 2100 block of 102nd Avenue in Oakland, CA about 10:15 p.m., they were approached by two unkown males. One of the males pulled out a firearm and hit the Applicant's spouse in the mouth with the firearm while she was holding their daughter, █████ in her arms.

The same male demanded her possessions. The Applicant's spouse was too afraid to react so she gave this male her purse, debit card, and I phone. The Applicant did not have enough time to protect his spouse because the 2nd male approached the Applicant and started to punch and kick him and subsequently demanded his belongings. The Applicant gave the male his I phone and I watch as he also had a firearm pointed directly at him.

After the Applicant and his spouse were beaten and robbed the Applicant and his spouse, with an injury to their child, as well, the males fled Eastbound on Bankroft Avenue. The two males had stolen the Applicant spouse's purse, debit card, two cellular phones, and one I watch. The Applicant had call the police

[2] The Interim Rule defines physical or mental abuse as "**injury or harm to the victim's physical person, or harm to or impairment of the emotional or psychological soundness of the victim.**" Interim Rule p. 23018; see also, 8 CFR 214.14(a)(8). In determining the existence of physical or mental abuse a "***wide range of physical or mental harm***" **is considered**. Interim Rule. P. 53018.

immediately and when the police arrived, the Applicant filed a report with them. The Applicant, his spouse, and his daughter were trasported to the hospital to be examined for their injuries sustained in the criminal act. The criminal investigation report was filed under Report number 18-004869.

The Applicant did everything he could to help the Oakland Police Department department in the apprehension of the persons who committed this crime. The Applicant and his spouse answered all their questions and made themselves available to be called at anytime by the Oakland Police in order to apprehend the persons who committed this crime. Lt. Rosin, of the Oakland Police Department, wrote the Applicant's spouse a letter stating the efforts that were being done to catch the persons who committed this crime (Please see **Exhibit 9**).

Please see **Exhibit 1,** Applicant stated below about the above mentioned crime:

> *"On January 27, 2018, approximately 3:00 p.m., my family and I went to visit my cousin and her family in Oakland, CA. We had spent the whole day there while all the children were playing. We had let our sons sleep over at my cousin's house. We had left the house around 10:15 p.m. when we realized that we had left our baby bottle at the house. We drove back to the house on Bancroft avenue when we noticed a honda accord parked there. As we were walking toward the house on the 2100 block of 102nd avenue approximately at 10:15 p.m. when we were approached by two males we did not know. One of the males pulled out a firearm and hit my wife, , in the mouth with his fists while she was holding our young daughter, in her arms.The same male demanded her possessions. My wife was too afraid to react so she gave this male her purse, debit card, and Iphone."*
>
> *"The incident happened so quickly. I didn't have enough time to respond and protect my wife and child because the second male approached me and started to kick and punch me several times demanding my belongings. Since they had firearms pointed at us, and was afraid that either I, my wife, or my children may have gotten shot, I gave this second male my Iphone and I watch. After they had beaten and robbed us, the two males then fled eastbound on Bancroft Avenue."*

III.
APPLICANT IS THE VICTIM OF THE CRIME

The crime discussed above falls under the U Visa statutes and the Applicant herein is a victim of this crime.

A victim of qualifying criminal activity means: (i) a person who has suffered direct and proximate harm as a result of the commission of one of the criminal acts named in the statute [A direct victim may include a witness to the crime who had a severe reaction such as a miscarriage or heart attack, see 72 FR 53014, 53017 (Sept. 17, 2007)] or (ii) "indirect victim" family members where the direct victim is deceased due to murder or manslaughter or is incompetent or incapacitated and where the family is the spouse and children under 21, and if the direct victim was under 21, his or her siblings under 18 and parents as well as spouse and children; or (iii) where the person is the victim of witness tampering, obstruction of justice or perjury, including attempt, solicitation or conspiracy to commit one or more of those offenses if he or she has been directly and proximately harmed by the perpetrator of those crimes and the perpetrator committed them as a means to avoid or frustrate efforts to investigate, arrest, prosecute or otherwise bring to justice the perpetrator for other criminal activity or to further the perpetrator's abuse or exploitation of or undue control over the petitioner. 8 C.F.R. §214.14(a)(14). See also 72 FR 53014, 53017 (Sept. 17, 2007). Here, in this case, the Applicant had pulled over the vehicle he was in to the curb to avoid any potential criminal

Physical or mental abuse means injury or harm to the victim's physical person, or harm to or impairment of the emotional or psychological soundness of the victim. 8 C.F.R. §214.14(a)(8); 72 FR at 53018. Factors considered include: the nature of the injury; the severity of the perpetrator's conduct; the severity of the harm; the duration of the infliction of harm; any permanent or serious harm to appearance, health and physical or mental soundness, and any aggravation of a victim's preexisting conditions. No single factor is required and a series of acts may suffice, even where no single act meets the standard. 8 C.F.R. §214.14(b)(1).

Therefore, based upon the above discussion, the Applicant is without doubt a victim of the enumerated crimes. (Please see **Exhibits 1, 2, 8, and 9).**

IV.
THE CRIMINAL ACTIVITY THAT VICTIMIZED APPLICANT OCCURRED IN THE UNITED STATES AND VIOLATED THE LAWS OF THE UNITED STATES

The victimization that Applicant endured occurred in California. Applicant was the victim of physical and mental assault in following crimes.

1. **Assault & Battery:** California Penal Code 242. Assault is an attempt to use force or violence on someone else. Battery, on the other hand, is the actual use of force or violence on someone else.

2. **Robbery:** Califonia Penal Code 211: Robbery is the felonious taking of personal property in the possession of another, from his person or immediate presence, and against his will, accomplished by means of force or fear.

3. **Willful Cruelty to a child:** Penal Code PC 273A(B): Any person who, under circumstances or conditions other than those likely to produce great bodily harm or death, willfully causes or permits any child to suffer, or inflicts thereon unjustifiable physical pain or mental suffering, or having the car of custody of any child, willfully causes or permits the person or health of that child to be injured or willfully causes or permits that child to be placed in a situation where his or her person or health may be endangered, is guilty of a misdemeanor.

The requirements of the three above stated criminal acts has been fulfilled in the criminal acts perpetrated against the Applicant by the persons who committed this crime (Please see **Exhibits 1, 2, 8, and 9**).

V.
APPLICANT SUFFERED SUBSTANTIAL PHYSICAL AND MENTAL ABUSE RESULTING FROM THE CRIMINAL ACTIVITY

In determining whether an applicant has suffered "substantial physical or mental abuse" USCIS must consider both the severity of the abuse inflicted by the perpetrator and severity of the injury suffered by the victim. Physical or mental abuse means injury or harm to the victim's physical person, or harm to or impairment of the emotional or psychological soundness of the victim. 8 C.F.R. § 214.14(a)(8); 72 FR at 53018. Factors considered include: the nature of the injury; the severity of the perpetrator's conduct; the severity of the harm; the duration of the infliction of harm; any permanent or serious harm to appearance, health and physical or mental soundness, and any aggravation of a victim's preexisting conditions. No single factor is required and a series of acts may suffice, even where no single act meets the standard. 8 C.F.R. § 214.14(b)(1). It is respectfully submitted that the arguments herein, and the supporting declarations and the documents that are attached all point to the conclusion that there has been substantial physical and mental abuse because of the being a victim of this criminal activity.

Evidence may include "reports and affidavits from police, judges, other court officials, medical personnel, school officials, clergy, social workers, and other social service agency personnel." Additionally, a combination of documents such as a photograph of the visibly injured applicants supported by affidavits of individuals who have personal knowledge of the facts regarding the criminal activity may be relevant as well. Ombudsman, USCIS Teleconference, "U Visa: One Year After the Interim Final Rule, #9 (Aug. 26, 2008).

In sum, applicant may be able to demonstrate the physical and mental abuse in the aggregate even if individual events might not be sufficient. *Matter of* (AAO Apr. 7, 2011). While it is submitted that the officer herein does not even need to look at the totality of the circumstances due to the fact there has been clear physical and emotional abuse as a result of this crime, it is put forth that using the totality of the circumstances will undoubtedly show this element of the U Visa requirements has been met.

Here, Applicant has suffered the requisite mental and physical abuse resulting from the criminal activity and he was a victim of, and is therefore eligible for U Nonimmigrant Status. **(See Exhibits 1 and 2).**

As per the Psychological Report of the Applicant (Please **see Exhibit 2)** , according to Dr. Marciano, the symptoms of the Applicant that are consistent with Generalized Anxiety Disorder which is when a person worries excessively about a variety of everyday problems for at least 6 month. Dr. Marciano states that the Applicant has experienced these systems for the past 6 months, consistent with the time of the incident in question. Dr. Marciano also states that the Applicant has been experiencing symptoms such as persistent, excessive, unrealistic, and uncontrollable worry about everyday life activities which is consistent with her diagnosis of Generalized Anxiety Disorder.

Dr. Marciano states that the above mentioned symptoms hinder his ability to function with normal daily activities and maintain a healthy and bonding relationship with others. (Please see **Exhibits 1 and 2).** The attached psychological report clearly indicates that it was this criminal incident that is the cause of the Applicant's s current psychological problems. (Please see **Exhibit 2**).

Dr. Marciano states that the Applicant also suffers from Post Traumatic Stress Disorder (PTSD). PTSD commonly occurs when an individual is faced with a traumatic event that threatens their safety or makes them feel helpless, such as in the Applicant's case (Please see **Exhibit 2).**

Dr. Celina Marciano has concluded that Applicant has been experiencing trauma symptoms for the past 6 months due to the assault incident. She also concludes that the fear the Applicant experienced, as he was confronted and threatened with a deadly weapon, he repeatedly articulated the incident as the main source of his psychological symptoms. (Please see **Exhibit 2**).

Finally, Dr. Marciano has stated that the Applicant has expressed genuine fear in an honest and forthright manner. She found that the Applicant to be credible and there were no signs of falsification and or exaggeration of the truth or facts. See Psychological Evaluation report, (Please see **Exhibit 2).**

VI.
APPLICANT POSSESSES INFORMATION CONCERNING THE CRIMINAL ACTIVITY

The I-918 Supplement B, U Nonimmigrant Status Certification signed by Lieutenant James P BEERE, Lieutenant of Police SVS of the Oakland Police Department. The Applicant was helpful in the investigation of the criminal activity, even after the incident occurred in trying to help the Police identify the persons who committed this crime. The Applicant and his spouse answered all the questions the police asked them concerning the crime and the Applicant and his spouse made themselves available to answer any other questions any time or to help the police officers in any way they needed (Please see **Exhibit 8** and **Form 918 Supplement B** for U Nonimmigrant Status Certification).

VII.
APPLICANT IS SUBMITTING EVERYTHING THAT IS NECESSARY FOR THE PROPER ADJUDICATION OF THIS PETITION

The I-918 must contain: (1) a signed statement by the petitioner describing the facts of the victimization; (2) any additional evidence demonstrating victimization including proof of physical or mental abuse; (3) an I-192 waiver pursuant to INA §212(d)(14) and 8 C.F.R. §212.17 if the petitioner is inadmissible and the proper certification. The attached Form I-192 with supporting documentation is attached. The proper certification must also be attached (see Section VIII, infra). A petitioner who previously received interim relief may submit Form I-918 without supporting evidence, 8 C.F.R. §214.14(c)(1), but USCIS is not bound by its previous determination. 8 C.F.R. §214.14(c)(4).

The burden is on the petitioner to demonstrate eligibility. 8 C.F.R. §214.14(c)(4). USCIS shall consider any credible evidence submitted to support the claim. INA §214(p)(4); 8 C.F.R. §214.14(c)(4). All items are properly within this petition including the requisite certification.

VIII.
APPLICANT SHOULD BE GRANTED WAIVER PURSUANT TO INA § 212(d)(14)

1. Waiver for U Visas pursuant to INA § 212(d)(14) In the Public or National Interest

The standard Congress set forth for granting U visa waivers under INA § 212(d)(14) was that a waiver may be granted if it is in the public or national interest. When U.S. Citizenship and Immigration Services (USCIS) issued its regulations in 2007, however, it did not provide specific guidance as to what that legal standard means or what particular factors USCIS would consider. This means that applicants must look to other types of waivers or language from Congress to determine what is in the national or public interest.

Many other waivers and benefits also use the language "public interest," including the INA § 209(c) waiver for asylees, Special Agricultural Workers applications, the J-1 hardship waiver, and parole. These benefits usually contain additional bases for approval, such as "humanitarian" reasons or the promotion of "family unity." In other words, "public interest" is only one factor or basis for granting these benefits. Most of these benefits are likely granted based on humanitarian reasons or to promote family unity, rather than in the public interest. Furthermore, consideration of the public interest tends to be a factor in all benefits or relief that require an exercise of discretion under the INA.

In a legalization case, the Board of Immigration Appeals (BIA) noted that "the term 'public interest' 'has been generally defined to mean something in which the public—the community at large—has some pecuniary interest, or some interest by which their legal rights or liabilities are affected."[3] And since there really is no set rule to determine what is in the public interest, that definition was adopted as appropriate in an attempt to define the public or national interest.[4] In the context of other benefits, little direct guidance is available regarding the factors that are taken into account to determine what is in the public interest.

The congressional record may provide some insight specific to the INA § 212(d)(14) waiver. Certainly, Congress believed that "strengthening the ability of law enforcement agencies to detect, investigate, and prosecute" crimes against immigrants without lawful status was in the public interest.12 It also determined that it was in the public interest to protect victims of those offenses, by providing some form of status to these victims. Thus, one could surmise that by providing a waiver with the only qualification being the public or national interest requirement, Congress wanted greater weight put on the interest of the public in arresting and prosecuting individuals who perpetrate crimes, and on providing status to victims of crimes. Congress must have wanted the standard applied to this waiver to be different and less burdensome than that applied to other waivers, otherwise Congress would have created a different standard, or required U visa petitioners to request a waiver under another INA § 212 waiver category.

The 2007 regulations, however, narrowed the scope and liberalness of the waiver in many ways. Even though the statutory intent was to have a standard liberal enough to comport with the humanitarian objectives of the government and the interests of law enforcement to be able to work with immigrants to prosecute crimes, USCIS in its regulations limited when a waiver is to be approved, and created a three-tier system for determining whether a waiver will be granted.

---

3 *Matter of P*, 19 I&N Dec. 823, 828 [Board of Immigration Appeals] (BIA 1988) (citing *Black's Law Dictionary*).

4 Id

- **Heightened Standard for Criminal and Security Grounds**

In addition to the mere public interest standard set forth by INA § 212(d)(14), USCIS has created two additional standards that it will apply to criminal offenses, thus creating three separate standards to the U waiver. First, USCIS requests more evidence related to discretion for waivers of criminal or related grounds.[5] Among the factors it will consider here are the number and severity of the offenses.[6] USCIS has also set forth a "general rule" that it will "only exercise favorable discretion in U nonimmigrant status cases in which a waiver for violent or dangerous crimes or the security and related grounds under Section 212(a)(3) of the Act is requested, in extraordinary circumstances."[7] USCIS reasons that such a standard is appropriate since it is within its discretion to even grant a visa.[8]

- **Evidence for the INA § 212(d)(14) Waiver**

When preparing evidence for the INA § 212(d)(14) waiver, it is useful to regard the waiver as having three separate standards. For most grounds of inadmissibility, applicant should provide evidence demonstrating that it is within the public and national interest for the waiver to be granted. The second standard is much more strict and applies to crimes and other offenses. Here, USCIS likely will apply a balancing test, as delineated in *Mendez-Moralez*.[9] The third standard is the strictest, following Matter of Jean,[10] and applies to violent or dangerous crimes or security and related grounds. This is the "extraordinary circumstances" standard.

To overcome criminal grounds, the foreign national must present certified copies of the criminal records along with sufficient evidence to allow "the adjudicator [to] balance adverse factors evidencing inadmissibility . . . with the social and humane considerations presented" and exercise discretion in applicant's favor. As with *Mendez-Moralez*,[11] in cases dealing with INA § 212 (c) waivers and cancellation of removal, the BIA has provided factors that may be considered in the exercise of favorable discretion. These include

- Family ties in the United States;
- Length of residence in the country;
- Hardship to applicant or family members;
- Employment history;
- Property or business ties;
- Value and service to the community;
- Evidence of rehabilitation for past crimes; and
- Other evidence of good character.[12]

---

[5] 8 [Code of Federal Regulations] CFR §212.17(b)(2).

[6] Id.

[7] 72 FR 53014, 53021 (Sept. 17, 2007); see also 8 CFR §212.17(b)(2)

[8] 72 FR 53014, at 53021.

[9] Matter of Mendez-Moralez, 21 I&N Dec. 296 (BIA 1996).

[10] Matter of Jean, 23 I&N Dec. 373 (AG 2002).

[11] Mendez-Moralez, 21 I&N Dec. 296.

[12] See Matter of Marin, 16 I&N Dec. 581, 584 (BIA 1978); see also Matter of C-V-T-, 22 I&N Dec 7 (BIA 1998).

USCIS will not exercise favorable discretion on those waivers without additional evidence of rehabilitation and factors related to discretion.[13] Considering the U visa waiver to be like an "extreme hardship" waiver could be helpful in cases with criminal grounds.

2. Applicant should be granted waiver pursuant to INA § 212(d)(14).

a. Applicant may be inadmissible pursuant to INA § 212 (a)(9)(C)(i)(I).

Applicant was born on November 20, 1989 in Guadalajara, Jalisco, Mexico (Please **see Exhibit 5).** Applicant's first entry into the United States was in 2004. The Applicant left the United States on January 3, 2011 after signing a voluntary departure document. The Applicant tried to enter the United States on July 16, 2011 but was turned back and he had to go back to Mexico. During the same week, in July of 2011, the Applicant entered the United States in the back of a friends car, and has been residing in the United State since then. The Applicant has resided in the United States for seven year now.

b. Applicant may be inadmissible pursuant to INA § 212 (a)(2)(A)(i).

Applicant has resided in the United States for more than 1 year under Unlawful Status, therefore he may be inadmissible pursuant to INA § 212 (a)(2)(A)(i). However, there is no delineated definition exists within the law for "crime of moral turpitude," though the term "moral turpitude" has been held to involve acts demonstrating "baseness, vileness, and depravity" on the part of the perpetrator.[14]

In evaluating whether a particular crime involves moral turpitude, USCIS does not look at the underlying conduct of the applicant, but at the language in the criminal statute.[15] If the statute is broad or multi-sectional (a "divisible statute," in the parlance of the law), the courts will look at the record of conviction—*i.e.*, the "charge (indictment), plea, verdict, and sentence"—to determine whether the crime for which the person was convicted involved moral turpitude.[16] In April 2015, the U.S. Attorney General resolved a split in the circuit courts of appeal and upheld this traditional framework for analyzing whether a conviction is for a crime involving moral turpitude. This decision vacated a prior holding that allowed for evidence outside of the record of conviction to be considered in circumstances where the record of conviction is inconclusive on the issue of moral turpitude.[17]

To be inadmissible under the multiple criminal convictions provision, (1) a foreign national must have been convicted of two or more crimes (other than purely political offenses), and (2) the aggregate sentences to confinement must have been five years or more.[18] Under this ground, it is irrelevant whether the convictions occurred in a single trial, whether the offenses arose from a single scheme of misconduct, or whether they involved moral turpitude.

---

[13] See VSC Stakeholder's Meeting, Aug. 20, 2009.

[14] Matter of Franklin, 20 I&N Dec. 867 (BIA 1994), aff'd, 72 F.3d 571 (8th Cir. 1995).

[15] Matter of L-V-C-, 22 I&N Dec. 594 (BIA 1999).

[16] Matter of Velasquez-Herrera, 24 I&N Dec. 503 (BIA 2008).

[17] Matter of Silva-Trevino, 24 I&N Dec. 687 (A.G. 2008) vacated 26 I&N Dec. 550 (A.G. 2015).

[18] INA §212(a)(2)(B).

Applicant was convicted of assault with a deadly weapon and the willful damage of the property of another on October 11, 2010. The Applicant has not any other charges since then and has tried to become a good citizen and has not incurred any other convictions since 2010 (Please see **Exhibit 11**).

Additionally, Applicant has not been charged for any serious crime as compared to violent and dangerous crime. Following crimes have been found to be violent or dangerous:

- Manslaughter[19];
- Reckless endangerment conviction from exchanging gunfire[20];
- Sexual molestation[21];
- Burglary[22]; and
- Felony substantial battery with a deadly weapon.[23]

On January 3, 2011, the Applicant signed a voluntary departure document and left the United States. On July 16, 2011, the Applicant entered tried to enter the United States without the proper documentation and was returned to Mexico on the same day. During the same week, the Applicant reentered the United States in the back of a car and has resided in the United States since that time. The Applicant was also convicted of the crimes listed above but has not committed any crime since 2010. The Applicant has reformed himself and has become a model citizen, husband, and parent since his last entry into the United States. There is no harm to the country in granting the waiver, because Respondent has genuinely made every attempt to work hard and become a productive member of society. Applicant has demonstrated that he is an upstanding member of his community, who has worked hard to remain a good and productive citizen.

a. **Applicant's waiver application should granted on humanitarian grounds.**

USCIS, has applied the factors articulated in *Matter of Marin* to criminal grounds of inadmissibility in U visa waiver cases.[24] As discussed below, applicants will need to provide sufficient evidence of these positive factors to overcome the negative ones that stem from the crime(s) and immigration violations.

The standard for evaluating the impact of violent or dangerous crimes on approvability comes from *Matter of Jean*.[25] In *Jean*, the attorney general (AG) reviewed whether Melanie Beaucejour Jean should have been granted a § 209(c) waiver. Jean came to the United States as a refugee in 1994. In 1995, Jean pled guilty to second-degree manslaughter after severely physically abusing a child in her care. After being released from jail, Jean tried to adjust her status and was put in removal proceedings.Her case went twice in front of an immigration judge and was reversed twice on appeal by the BIA. After the second appeal, the AG decided to review the case.

---

[19] Matter of Jean, 23 I&N Dec. 373 (AG 2002).
[20] Victor v. AG, 2010 U.S. App. LEXIS 15674 (3d Cir. 2010) (unpublished).
[21] Mejia v. Gonzales, 499 F.3d 991 (9th Cir. 2007).
[22] Pimentel v. Mukasey, 530 F.3d 321 (5th Cir. 2008).
[23] Ali v. Achim, 468 F.3d 462 (7th Cir. 2006).
[24] 72 FR at 53021.
[25] Matter of Jean, 23 I&N Dec. 373 (AG 2002).

The AG criticized the BIA's determination that Jean had qualified for a waiver because the BIA had looked only at the emotional hardship the family would endure if Jean were removed.[26] The BIA did not weigh or balance the hardship against negative factors, specifically Jean's crime. The AG determined that evaluations of waivers "cannot ... focus solely on family hardships, but must consider the nature of the criminal offense that rendered a foreign national inadmissible in the first place." He further held that, in situations such as Jean's, the balance "will nearly always" require a denial of the waiver. Only in certain "extraordinary circumstances" will the waiver be granted, though "such a showing might still be insufficient."

The most difficult grounds of inadmissibility to overcome are those related to violent and dangerous crimes and the security-related grounds. Here, USCIS will exercise favorable discretion only in "extraordinary circumstances" under the balancing standard discussed above in Matter of Jean.[27] The AG stated that national security, foreign policy considerations, or exceptional and extremely unusual hardship would all constitute an "extraordinary circumstance." In some cases, however, such a showing would not be enough to merit favorable discretion.

If the crime is clearly a violent or a dangerous one, then applicant must show "extraordinary circumstances" have been met. For most applicants, this will mean showing exceptional or extremely unusual hardship. This is also the standard that is used in cancellation of removal for non–lawful permanent residents under INA § 240A(b)(1). The BIA analyzed this requirement in Matter of Monreal,[28] and held that the factors to determine whether "exceptional or extremely unusual hardship" is met are the same as for "extreme hardship," even though in a cancellation case, only the hardship to the qualifying relative counts. It is reasonable to assume that in the U visa waiver case, the foreign national will be able to demonstrate "exceptional or extremely unusual hardship" to him- or herself, given that in Matter of Jean,[29] the AG did not require a showing of hardship to a qualifying family member. The factors the BIA said it would consider include.

- *The age of applicant at the time of entry and when relief is requested;*

Applicant was 14-years-old when he entered the United States for the first time and currently he is 39-years-old.

- *Length of residence in the United States;*

Applicant has continuous residence in the United States for past 7 years.

- *Applicant's immigration history.*

The Applicant entered the United States for the first time in 2004 without inspection. In January of 2011, the Applicant signed a Voluntary Departure Document and left the United States for Mexico. He tried to enter the United States again in July of 2011 but did not have the proper documentation and was returned

26 Matter of Jean, 23 I&N Dec. 373, 382 (AG 2002).

27 Jean, 23 I&N Dec. 373

28 23 I&N Dec. 56 (BIA 2001).

29 Matter of Jean, 23 I&N Dec. 373 (AG 2002).

to Mexico. During the same week, the Applicant entered the United States for the last time in July of 2011, and he has continuously resided in the United States for the last 7 years and has not had any other immigration proceedings.

- *Political and economic conditions in applicant's home country;*

Applicant has been reading news of the violence and high levels of crimes in Mexico, due to which he is not willing to leave his home in the United States. In addition, living conditions in Mexico are not as good as they are in the United States. Mexico is considered to be a highly volatile country in which to live due to its increasing drug cartel activity and increasing arrests. The country has undergone major political change in the past years, and the resulting economic and political turmoil has brought with it soaring crime rates, a growing drug trafficking problem, and burgeoning organized crime. (Please see **Exhibits 14-19).**

Mexico has experienced increasingly high health problems due to inadequate medical facilities. The country's great economic polarization has stimulated criminal activity in the lower socioeconomic strata, which include the majority of the country's population.

Please see **Exhibit 14,** World Report 2017: Mexico-Human Rights Watch, The relevant part is stated below:

> *"According to a survey of more than 64,000 people incarcerated in 370Mexican prisons located throughout the country in 2016, performed by Mexico's national statistics office (Instituto Nacional de Estadística y Geografía – INEGI), 57.8 percent of the prison population reported having suffered some type of physical violence at the time of their arrest. Of these people, 19 percent reported receiving electrical shocks; 36 percent being choked, held underwater, or smothered; and 59 percent being hit or kicked. In addition, 28 percent reported that they were threatened that their family would be harmed."*

> *"The criminal justice system routinely fails to provide justice to victims of violent crimes and human rights violations. Causes of failure include corruption, inadequate training and resources, and complicity of prosecutors and public defenders with criminals and abusive officials. The failure of law enforcement has contributed to the emergence of armed citizen self-defense groups in several parts of the country."*

Please also see **Exhibit 15**, Amnesty International - Mexico Annual Report 2017/2018. The relevant part is stated below:

> *"Violence increased throughout Mexico. The armed forces continued to undertake regular policing functions. Human rights defenders and journalists were threatened, attacked and killed; digital attacks and surveillance were particularly common. Widespread arbitrary detentions continued to lead to torture and other ill-treatment, enforced disappearances and extrajudicial executions. Impunity persisted for human rights violations and crimes under international law. Mexico received a record number of asylum claims, mostly from nationals of El Salvador, Honduras, Guatemala and Venezuela. Violence against women remained a*

major concern; new data showed that two thirds of women had experienced gender-based violence during their lives. The rights to housing and education were compromised by two major earthquakes. robbery in various Mexican states. This Travel Warning replaces the Travel Warning for Mexico, issued April 15, 2016."

"Gender-based violence against women and girls was widespread. Most of the cases were inadequately investigated and perpetrators enjoyed impunity. Sufficient and current data on gender-based killings was not available. However, official data for 2016 was published indicating that 2,668 women were considered to be victims of homicide, pending further investigations. In August, the National Institute of Statistics and Geography published a survey estimating that 66.1% of girls and women aged 15 or above had experienced gender-based violence at least once in their lives, and that 43.5% of women had experienced gender-based violence committed by their partners."

Please also see **Exhibit 16**, U.S. Department of State - Mexico Travel Advisory 2018 - Mexico Annual Report 2017/2018. The relevant part is stated below:

"Exercise increased caution in Mexico due to crime. Some areas have increased risk. Read he entire Travel Advisory. Violent crime, such as homicide, kidnapping, carjacking, and robbery, is widespread. The U.S. government has limited ability to provide emergency services to U.S. citizens in many areas of Mexico as U.S. government employees are prohibited from travel to these areas. U.S. government employees are prohibited from intercity travel after dark in many areas of Mexico. U.S. government employees are also not permitted to drive from the U.S.-Mexico border to or from the interior parts of Mexico with the exception of daytime travel on Highway 15 between Nogales and Hermosillo."

"Do not travel due to crime. Violent crime, such as murder, armed robbery, carjacking, kidnapping, extortion, and sexual assault, is common. Gang activity, including gun battles, is widespread. Armed criminal groups target public and private passenger buses traveling through Tamaulipas, often taking passengers hostage and demanding ransom payments. Local law enforcement has limited capability to respond to violence in many parts of the state."

The Applicant also needs to stay in the United States because of the socioeconomic conditions in the country of Mexico. Applicant lives with and provides for his wife and their three children. If Applicant is sent back to Mexico, his wife and children will not have anybody to support them and they will become homeless and will not be able to take care of themselves. The Applicant has not been back to Mexico for over 7 years and is extremely fearful for his safety as he has no place to live, no job, and no money to support himself in Mexico.

Please **see Exhibit 18**. According to Mexico 2017 Crime & Safety Report: Mexico City - OSAC, the relevant part is stated below:

> *"The general crime rate in Mexico City is above the U.S. national average, and crime varies widely. Armed robberies, kidnappings, car thefts, credit card fraud, and various forms of residential/street crime are daily concerns. Thefts of the vehicle's operating computer and sound systems are also common crimes. The low rate of criminal convictions contributes to the high rate of crime. Although Mexico employs strict gun-control laws, criminals are often armed with handguns (or knives). Although there is no pattern of criminals specifically targeting foreign or American businesses/personnel, criminals will target anyone perceived as lucrative and vulnerable. Criminals select victims based on an appearance of prosperity, vulnerability, or a lack of awareness."*

The Applicant is afraid that he will be recognized as an American as soon as he enters his country since he hasn't been back to Mexico in over 7 years. Despite the Applicant's past mistakes, he has completely reformed himself and has become a changed man in the last 7 years. Not only is the Applicant a person of high moral character and is a hard worker and would be recognized as such and victimized as soon as he entered Mexico. There would be considerable danger for the Applicant if he was sent back to his country.

Applicant is a person who would suffer hardship if he was forced to relocate outside the United States. Granting Applicant, a waiver necessary for the U visa is in the public interest generally because local law enforcement use of U visas sends a crucial message to immigrants that they can report crime and to perpetrators that they cannot victimize immigrants with impunity. A waiver in this case furthers that public benefit and American humanitarian values because Applicant assisted, and continues to assist, local authorities in the persecution of the perpetrator of the crime.

As the exhibits and information in this petition shows, the Applicant has resided continuously in the United States for over 7 years without ever leaving the United States. The Applicant has been present in the United States in Unlawful Status for more than 1 year. However, the whole purpose of the regulations waiving grounds of inadmissibility is to allow persons who were victims of crime to be able to obtain the U Visa.

The legislative intent of the allowing waivers in the U Visa application shows that the burden needed for granting those waivers is considerably less than those needed for other types of applications such as an adjustment of status application. In fact, many crimes and grounds of inadmissibility which are not waivable in other areas of immigration are not only waivable when submitted with the U Visa Petition, but the burden of showing hardship on the applicant is much less.

Clearly, the intent of allowing this is directly related to the fact that the government wanted victims of crime to be able to obtain the U Visa and to not be denied that ability. Here, this applicant was a victim of a severe crime. This is a case whereby the victim of this crime and the seriousness of that crime and his continuing cooperation with the government should clearly outweigh any grounds of inadmissibility.

His suffering through the years because he is a victim of this heinous crime should be a large factor in granting the waiver of all the grounds of inadmissibility. Thus, when taken as a whole, it is respectfully submitted that this applicant has met the necessary burden to show his grounds of inadmissibility should be waived.

IX.

CONCLUSION

Based on the above, Applicant respectfully requests that discretion be exercised favorably in his case and that the Service grant U Nonimmigrant Status and waiver to him.

If you need any information, please do not hesitate to call at 562-495-0554. Thank you for your kind consideration in this matter.

Regards,

Brian D. Lerner
Attorney at Law

FORMS

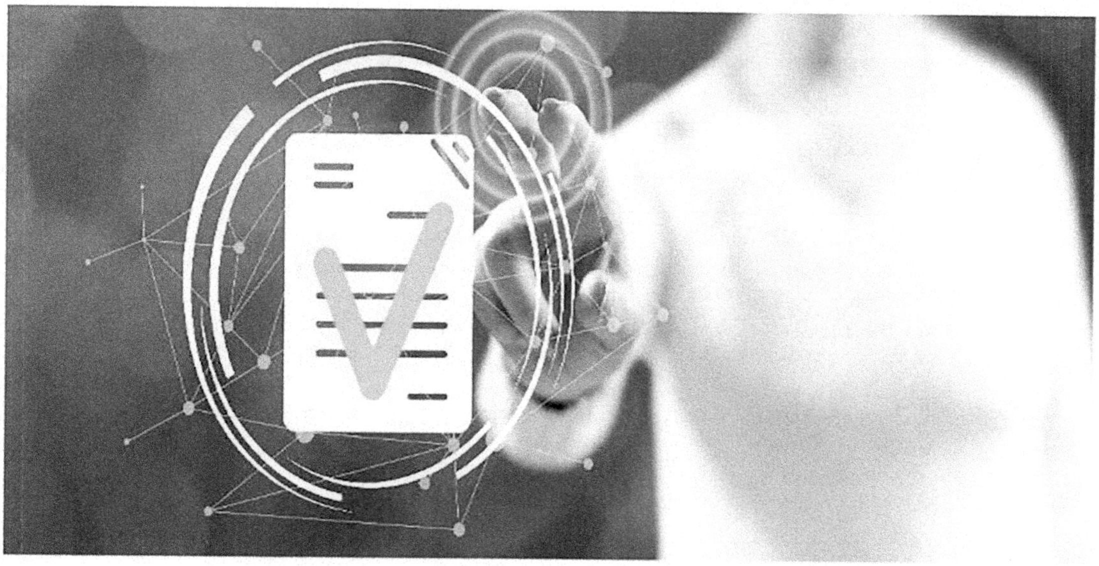

e-Notification of Application/Petition Acceptance

Department of Homeland Security
U.S. Citizenship and Immigration Services

USCIS
Form G-1145

What Is the Purpose of This Form?

Use this form to request an electronic notification (e-Notification) when U.S. Citizenship and Immigration Services accepts your immigration application. This service is available for applications filed at a USCIS Lockbox facility.

General Information

Complete the information below and clip this form to the first page of your application package. You will receive one e-mail and/or text message for each form you are filing.

We will send the e-Notification within 24 hours after we accept your application. Domestic customers will receive an e-mail and/or text message; overseas customers will only receive an e-mail. Undeliverable e-Notifications cannot be resent.

The e-mail or text message will display your receipt number and tell you how to get updated case status information. It will not include any personal information. The e-Notification does not grant any type of status or benefit; rather it is provided as a convenience to customers.

USCIS will also mail you a receipt notice (I-797C), which you will receive within 10 days after your application has been accepted; use this notice as proof of your pending application or petition.

USCIS Privacy Act Statement

AUTHORITIES: The information requested on this form is collected pursuant to section 103(a) of the Immigration and Nationality Act, as amended INA section 101, et seq.

PURPOSE: The primary purpose for providing the information on this form is to request an electronic notification when USCIS accepts immigration form. The information you provide will be used to send you a text and/or email message.

DISCLOSURE: The information you provide is voluntary. However, failure to provide the requested information may prevent USCIS from providing you a text and/or email message receipting your immigration form.

ROUTINE USES: The information provided on this form will be used by and disclosed to DHS personnel and contractors in accordance with approved routine uses, as described in the associated published system of records notices [DHS/USCIS-007 - Benefits Information System and DHS/USCIS-001 - Alien File (A-File) and Central Index System (CIS), which can be found at www.dhs.gov/privacy]. The information may also be made available, as appropriate for law enforcement purposes or in the interest of national security.

Complete this form and clip it on top of the first page of your immigration form(s).

Applicant/Petitioner Full Last Name	Applicant/Petitioner Full First Name	Applicant/Petitioner Full Middle Name

Email Address	Mobile Phone Number (Text Message)
[APPLICANT]	(650) 438-6091

Notice of Entry of Appearance as Attorney or Accredited Representative

Department of Homeland Security

DHS Form G-28
OMB No. 1615-0105
Expires 03/31/2018

Part 1. Information About Attorney or Accredited Representative

1. USCIS ELIS Account Number (*if any*) ▶

Name and Address of Attorney or Accredited Representative

2.a. Family Name (*Last Name*): Lerner
2.b. Given Name (*First Name*): Brian
2.c. Middle Name: David
3.a. Street Number and Name: 3233 E Broadway
3.b. Apt. ☐ Ste. ☐ Flr. ☐
3.c. City or Town: Long Beach
3.d. State: CA 3.e. ZIP Code: 90803
3.f. Province:
3.g. Postal Code:
3.h. Country: USA
4. Daytime Telephone Number: 5624950554
5. Fax Number: 5626088672
6. E-Mail Address (*if any*): blerner@californiaimmigration.us
7. Mobile Telephone Number (*if any*):

Part 2. Notice of Appearance as Attorney or Accredited Representative

This appearance relates to immigration matters before (*Select **only one** box*):

1.a. ☒ USCIS
1.b. List the form numbers: I-192 I-765 I-918 I918B
2.a. ☐ ICE
2.b. List the specific matter in which appearance is entered:
3.a. ☐ CBP
3.b. List the specific matter in which appearance is entered:

I enter my appearance as attorney or accredited representative at the request of:

4. Select **only one** box:
☒ Applicant ☐ Petitioner ☐ Requestor
☐ Respondent (ICE, CBP)

Information About Applicant, Petitioner, Requestor, or Respondent

5.a. Family Name (*Last Name*): [redacted]
5.b. Given Name (*First Name*): [redacted]
5.c. Middle Name: Arturo
6. Name of Company or Organization (*if applicable*):

Part 2. Notice of Appearance as Attorney or Accredited Representative *(continued)*

Information About Applicant, Petitioner, Requestor, or Respondent (continued)

7. USCIS ELIS Account Number *(if any)* ►

8. Alien Registration Number (A-Number) or Receipt Number

9. Daytime Telephone Number: 6504386091

10. Mobile Telephone Number *(if any)*: 6504386091

11. E-Mail Address *(if any)*

Mailing Address of Applicant, Petitioner, Requestor, or Respondent

NOTE: Provide the mailing address of the applicant, petitioner, requestor, or respondent. **Do not** provide the business mailing address of the attorney or accredited representative **unless** it serves as the safe mailing address on the application, petition, or request being filed with this Form G-28.

12.a. Street Number and Name: 533 3rd Avenue

12.b. Apt. ☐ Ste. ☐ Flr. ☐

12.c. City or Town: San Bruno

12.d. State: CA **12.e.** ZIP Code: 94066

12.f. Province

12.g. Postal Code

12.h. Country: USA

Part 3. Eligibility Information for Attorney or Accredited Representative

Select **all applicable** items.

1.a. ☒ I am an attorney eligible to practice law in, and a member in good standing of, the bar of the highest courts of the following states, possessions, territories, commonwealths, or the District of Columbia. *(If you need additional space, use* ***Part 6.****)*

Licensing Authority: Supreme Court of California

1.b. Bar Number *(if applicable)*

1.c. Name of Law Firm: Law Offices of Brian D. Lerner

1.d. I *(choose one)* ☒ ***am not*** ☐ ***am***

subject to any order of any court or administrative agency disbarring, suspending, enjoining, restraining, or otherwise restricting me in the practice of law. If you are subject to any orders, explain in the space below. *(If you need additional space, use* ***Part 6.****)*

2.a. ☐ I am an accredited representative of the following qualified nonprofit religious, charitable, social service, or similar organization established in the United States, so recognized by the Department of Justice, Board of Immigration Appeals, in accordance with 8 CFR 292.2. Provide the name of the organization and the expiration date of accreditation.

2.b. Name of Recognized Organization

2.c. Date accreditation expires *(mm/dd/yyyy)* ►

Part 3. Eligibility Information for Attorney or Accredited Representative *(continued)*

3. ☐ I am associated with

the attorney or accredited representative of record who previously filed Form G-28 in this case, and my appearance as an attorney or accredited representative is at his or her request.

NOTE: If you select this item, also complete **Item Numbers 1.a. - 1.b. or Item Numbers 2.a. - 2.c.** in **Part 3.** *(whichever is appropriate).*

4.a. ☐ I am a law student or law graduate working under the direct supervision of the attorney or accredited representative of record on this form in accordance with the requirements in 8 CFR 292.1(a)(2)(iv).

4.b. Name of Law Student or Law Graduate

Part 4. Applicant, Petitioner, Requestor, or Respondent Consent to Representation, Contact Information, and Signature

Consent to Representation and Release of Information

1. I have requested the representation of and consented to being represented by the attorney or accredited representative named in **Part 1.** of this form. According to the Privacy Act of 1974 and DHS policy, I also consent to the disclosure to the named attorney or accredited representative of any record pertaining to me that appears in any system of records of USCIS, ICE or CBP.

When you (the applicant, petitioner, requestor, or respondent) are represented, DHS will send notices to both you and your attorney or accredited representative either through mail or electronic delivery.

DHS will also send the Form I-94, Arrival Departure Record, to you **unless** you select **Item Number 2.a.** in **Part 4.** All secure identity documents and Travel Documents will be sent to you (the applicant, petitioner, requestor, or respondent) at your U.S. mailing address **unless** you ask us to send your secure identity documents to your attorney of record or accredited representative.

If you do not want to receive original notices or secure identity documents directly, but would rather have such notices and documents sent to your attorney of record or accredited representative, please select **all applicable** boxes below:

2.a ☒ I request DHS send any notice (including Form I-94) on an application, petition, or request to the U.S. business address of my attorney of record or accredited representative as listed in this form. I understand that I may change this election at any future date through written notice to DHS.

2.b. ☐ I request that DHS send any secure identity document, such as a Permanent Resident Card, Employment Authorization Document, or Travel Document, that I am approved to receive and authorized to possess, to the U.S. business address of my attorney of record or accredited representative as listed in this form or to a designated military or diplomatic address for pickup in a foreign country (if permitted). I consent to having my secure identity document sent to my attorney of record or accredited representative's U.S. business address and understand that I may request, at any future date and through written notice to DHS, that DHS send any secure identity document to me directly.

3.a. Signature of Applicant, Petitioner, Requestor, or Respondent

➡

3.b. Date of Signature *(mm/dd/yyyy)* ►

Part 5. Signature of Attorney or Accredited Representative

I have read and understand the regulations and conditions contained in 8 CFR 103.2 and 292 governing appearances and representation before the Department of Homeland Security. I declare under penalty of perjury under the laws of the United States that the information I have provided on this form is true and correct.

1. Signature of Attorney or Accredited Representative

2. Signature of Law Student or Law Graduate

3. Date of Signature *(mm/dd/yyyy)* ►

Part 6. Additional Information

Use the space provided below to provide additional information pertaining to **Part 3., Item Numbers 1.a. - 1.d.** or to provide your U.S. business address for purposes of receiving secure identity documents for your client (if your client has consented to your receipt of such documents under **Part 4.**)

Application for Advance Permission to Enter as a Nonimmigrant

Department of Homeland Security
U.S. Citizenship and Immigration Services

USCIS
Form I-192
OMB No. 1615-0017
Expires 06/30/2018

For DHS Use Only	Received	Returned Trans. Out	Fee Stamp
	Trans. In	Completed	
	Action by the Department of Homeland Security		
	☐ Granted, subject to revocation at any time, upon the following terms and conditions:		Date of Action (mm/dd/yyyy) ______ DD or OIC ______ Office ______

To be completed by an attorney or accredited representative (if any).			
☒ Select this box if Form G-28 or Form G-28I is attached.	Volag Number	Attorney State Bar Number (if applicable)	Attorney or Accredited Representative USCIS ELIS Online Number (if any)

► **START HERE - Type or print in black ink.**

Part 1. Application Type

I am applying to the Secretary of Homeland Security for permission to enter the United States temporarily under the provisions of section 212(d)(3)(A)(ii), section 212(d)(13), or section 212(d)(14) of the Immigration and Nationality Act (INA).

I am seeking this permission so that I may obtain (Select **only one** box):

1. A. ☐ Admission as a nonimmigrant (other than as a T or U nonimmigrant)

   B. ☒ Status as a victim of trafficking (T nonimmigrant status) or a victim of a crime (U nonimmigrant status)

Part 2. Information About You

1. Family Name (Last Name) [redacted] Given Name (First Name) [redacted] Middle Name [redacted]
2. Alien Registration Number (A-Number) (if any)
3. USCIS Online Account Number (if any) ►
4. Date of Birth (mm/dd/yyyy) 11/20/1989
5. Place of Birth
   City or Town: Guadalajara
   State or Province: Jalisco
   Country: Mexico
6. Country of Citizenship or Nationality: Mexico

Part 2. Information About You (continued)

7. Physical Address

Street Number and Name | Apt. Ste. Flr. ☐ ☐ ☐ | Number

City or Town | State: CA | ZIP Code: 94066

Province | Postal Code | Country: USA

8. Provide the addresses where you have resided during the past five years, starting with the last place you lived prior to your current physical address listed under **Item Number 7.** If you need extra space to complete this section, use the space provided in **Part 7. Additional Information.**

A. Residence Number 1

Date of Residence From (mm/dd/yyyy) 07/16/2011 To (mm/dd/yyyy) Present

Street Number and Name | Apt. Ste. Flr. ☐ ☐ ☐ | Number

City or Town | State: CA | ZIP Code: 94066

Province | Postal Code | Country: USA

B. Residence Number 2

Date of Residence From (mm/dd/yyyy) | To (mm/dd/yyyy)

Street Number and Name | Apt. Ste. Flr. ☐ ☐ ☐ | Number

City or Town | State | ZIP Code

Province | Postal Code | Country

C. Residence Number 3

Date of Residence From (mm/dd/yyyy) | To (mm/dd/yyyy)

Street Number and Name | Apt. Ste. Flr. ☐ ☐ ☐ | Number

City or Town | State | ZIP Code

Province | Postal Code | Country

Part 2. Information About You (continued)

D. Residence Number 4

Date of Residence From (mm/dd/yyyy) [ ] To (mm/dd/yyyy) [ ]

Street Number and Name [ ] Apt. Ste. Flr. ☐ ☐ ☐ Number [ ]

City or Town [ ] State [ ] ZIP Code [ ]

Province [ ] Postal Code [ ] Country [ ]

Travel Information

9. Location at which you plan to enter the United States (desired Port-of-Entry)

City [ ] State [ ]

10. Name of Port-of-Entry [ ]

11. How do you plan to travel to the United States? (For example, by plane, ship, car) [ ]

12. When do you plan to enter the United States? (mm/dd/yyyy) [ ]

13. Approximate Length of Stay in the United States

Indefinitely

14. What is the purpose of your stay in the United States? Explain fully below.

I am waiting for U Visa status

Immigration and Criminal History

15. Do you believe that you may be inadmissible to the United States? ☒ Yes ☐ No

If you answered "Yes," explain the reasons why you believe, according to the best of your knowledge, that you may be inadmissible in **Part 7. Additional Information**. If you were told that you are inadmissible, provide the reason you were given.

16. Have you previously filed an application for advance permission to enter the United States as a nonimmigrant? ☐ Yes ☒ No

If you answered "Yes," provide the details in **Items A. - C.** in **Item Number 17.** If you need extra space to complete this section, use the space provided in **Part 7. Additional Information**.

17. A. Date Application Filed (mm/dd/yyyy) [ ]

B. Location where you filed your application (For example, U.S. Citizenship and Immigration Services (USCIS) Office or Port-of-Entry)

USCIS Office or U.S. Port-of-Entry

City or Town [ ] State or Province [ ] Country [ ]

Part 2. Information About You (continued)

NOTE: If you are an applicant for T nonimmigrant status or a petitioner for U nonimmigrant status, you do not need to answer Item Numbers 18. - 21.

18. Have you **EVER** been in the United States for a period of six months or more? ☐ Yes ☐ No

If you answered "Yes," provide the dates you were in the United States (from and to) and your immigration status at the time of entry into the United States in the space provided in **Part 7. Additional Information**.

19. Have you **EVER** filed an application or petition for immigration benefits with the U.S. Government, or has one ever been filed on your behalf? ☐ Yes ☐ No

If you answered "Yes" to **Item Number 19.** provide the information in the space provided in **Part 7. Additional Information.**

NOTE: If you (or somebody else on your behalf) have filed multiple applications or petitions for immigration benefits with the U.S. Government, use the space provided in **Part 7.** to also provide the following information:

A. Type of application or petition filed;

B. Location where you (or the other person) filed the application or petition (for example, USCIS office or Port-of-Entry);

C. Outcome of the application or petition (for example, approved, denied, or is pending)

20. Have you **EVER** been denied or refused an immigration benefit by the U.S. Government, or had a benefit revoked or terminated (including but not limited to visas)? ☐ Yes ☐ No

If you answered "Yes" to **Item Number 20.**, provide the information in the space provided in **Part 7. Additional Information.**

21. Have you **EVER**, in or outside the United States, been arrested, cited, charged, indicted, fined, convicted, or imprisoned for breaking or violating any law or ordinance, excluding minor traffic violations? If you answered "Yes," describe the incidents in detail and include all offenses where impaired driving may have been an issue in the space provided in **Part 7. Additional Information.** ☐ Yes ☐ No

Part 3. Biographic Information

1. Ethnicity (Select **only one** box) ☒ Hispanic or Latino ☐ Not Hispanic or Latino

2. Race (Select **all applicable** boxes)

☐ White ☐ Asian ☐ Black or African American ☐ American Indian or Alaska Native ☐ Native Hawaiian or Other Pacific Islander

3. Height Feet 5 Inches 7 **4.** Weight Pounds 1 6 5

5. Eye Color (Select **only one** box)

☐ Black ☐ Blue ☒ Brown ☐ Gray ☐ Green ☐ Hazel ☐ Maroon ☐ Pink ☐ Unknown/Other

6. Hair Color (Select **only one** box)

☐ Bald (No hair) ☒ Black ☐ Blond ☐ Brown ☐ Gray ☐ Red ☐ Sandy ☐ White ☐ Unknown/Other

Part 4. Applicant's Statement, Contact Information, Certification, and Signature

NOTE: Read the information on penalties in the **Penalties** section of the Form I-192 Instructions before completing this part.

NOTE: Select the box for either **Item A. or B.** in **Item Number 1.** If applicable, select the box for **Item Number 2.**

1. Applicant's Statement Regarding the Interpreter

   A. [X] I can read and understand English, and have read and understand every question and instruction on this application and my answer to every question.

   B. [ ] The interpreter named in **Part 5.** read to me every question and instruction on this application, and my answer to every question in __________, a language in which I am fluent, and I understood everything.

2. Applicant's Statement Regarding the Preparer

   [ ] At my request, the preparer named in **Part 6.**, Brian D. Lerner, prepared this application for me based only upon information I provided or authorized.

Applicant's Contact Information

3. Applicant's Daytime Telephone Number

4. Applicant's Mobile Telephone Number (if any)

5. Applicant's Email Address (if any)

Applicant's Certification

Copies of any documents I have submitted are exact photocopies of unaltered, original documents, and I understand that USCIS may require that I submit original documents to USCIS at a later date. Furthermore, I authorize the release of any information from any of my records that USCIS may need to determine my eligibility for the immigration benefit I seek.

I further authorize release of information contained in this application, in supporting documents, and in my USCIS records to other entities and persons where necessary for the administration and enforcement of U.S. immigration laws.

I understand that USCIS may require me to appear for an appointment to take my biometrics (fingerprints, photograph, and/or signature) and, at that time, if I am required to provide biometrics, I will be required to sign an oath reaffirming that:

1) I reviewed and provided or authorized all of the information in my application;
2) I understood all of the information contained in, and submitted with, my application; and
3) All of this information was complete, true, and correct at the time of filing.

I certify, under penalty of perjury, that I provided or authorized all of the information in my application, I understand all of the information contained in, and submitted with, my application, and that all of this information is complete, true, and correct.

Applicant's Signature

6. Applicant's Signature

Date of Signature (mm/dd/yyyy)

NOTE TO ALL APPLICANTS: If you do not completely fill out this application or fail to submit required documents listed in the Instructions, USCIS may deny your application.

Part 5. Interpreter's Contact Information, Certification, and Signature

Provide the following information about the interpreter.

Interpreter's Full Name

1. Interpreter's Family Name (Last Name)

   Interpreter's Given Name (First Name)

2. Interpreter's Business or Organization Name (if any)

Interpreter's Mailing Address

3. Street Number and Name

   Apt. Ste. Flr. Number

   City or Town

   State

   ZIP Code

   Province

   Postal Code

   Country

Interpreter's Contact Information

4. Interpreter's Daytime Telephone Number

5. Interpreter's Mobile Telephone Number (if any)

6. Interpreter's Email Address (if any)

Interpreter's Certification

I certify, under penalty of perjury, that:

I am fluent in English and ______, which is the same language specified in **Part 4.**, **Item B.** in **Item Number 1.**, and I have read to this applicant in the identified language every question and instruction on this application and his or her answer to every question. The applicant informed me that he or she understands every instruction, question, and answer on the application, including the **Applicant's Certification**, and has verified the accuracy of every answer.

Interpreter's Signature

7. Interpreter's Signature

   Date of Signature (mm/dd/yyyy)

Part 6. Contact Information, Declaration, and Signature of the Person Preparing this Application, if Other Than the Applicant

Provide the following information about the preparer.

Preparer's Full Name

1. Preparer's Family Name (Last Name): Lerner
   Preparer's Given Name (First Name): Brian

2. Preparer's Business or Organization Name (if any): Law Offices of Brian D. Lerner, APC

Preparer's Mailing Address

3. Street Number and Name: 3233 E. Broadway
   Apt. ☐ Ste. ☐ Flr. ☐ Number:
   City or Town: Long Beach
   State: CA
   ZIP Code: 90803
   Province:
   Postal Code:
   Country: USA

Preparer's Contact Information

4. Preparer's Daytime Telephone Number: (562) 495-0554

5. Preparer's Mobile Number (if any):

6. Preparer's Email Address (if any): blerner@californiaimmigration.us

Preparer's Statement

7. A. ☐ I am not an attorney or accredited representative but have prepared this application on behalf of the applicant and with the applicant's consent.

   B. ☒ I am an attorney or accredited representative and my representation of the applicant in this case ☒ extends ☐ does not extend beyond the preparation of this application.

   NOTE: If you are an attorney or accredited representative whose representation extends beyond preparation of this application, you may be obliged to submit a completed Form G-28, Notice of Entry of Appearance as Attorney or Accredited Representative, or G-28I, Notice of Entry of Appearance as Attorney In Matters Outside the Geographical Confines of the United States, with this application.

Preparer's Certification

By my signature, I certify, under penalty of perjury, that I prepared this application at the request of the applicant. The applicant then reviewed this completed application and informed me that he or she understands all of the information contained in, and submitted with, his or her application, including the **Applicant's Certification**, and that all of this information is complete, true, and correct. I completed this application based only on information that the applicant provided to me or authorized me to obtain or use.

Preparer's Signature

8. Preparer's Signature:
   Date of Signature (mm/dd/yyyy):

Part 7. Additional Information

If you need extra space to provide any additional information within this application, use the space below. If you need more space than what is provided, you may make copies of this page to complete and file with this application or attach a separate sheet of paper. Include your name and A-Number (if any) at the top of every sheet; indicate the **Page Number**, **Part Number**, and **Item Number** to which your answer refers; and sign and date each sheet.

1. Family Name (Last Name) [redacted] Given Name (First Name) [redacted] Middle Name [redacted]

2. A-Number (if any) ► A- [redacted]

3. A. Page Number: 3 B. Part Number: 2 C. Item Number: 15

   D. **I believe I am inadmissible because I have lived in the United States for more than a year under unlawful status**

4. A. Page Number B. Part Number C. Item Number

   D.

5. A. Page Number B. Part Number C. Item Number

   D.

6. A. Page Number B. Part Number C. Item Number

   D.

Application For Employment Authorization

Department of Homeland Security
U.S. Citizenship and Immigration Services

USCIS Form I-765
OMB No. 1615-0040
Expires 02/28/2018

For USCIS Use Only	Fee Stamp	Action Block	Initial Receipt	Resubmitted
			Relocated	
			Received	Sent
			Completed	
☐ Application Approved ☐ Authorization/Extension Valid From ______ ☐ Authorization/Extension Valid To ______		☐ Application Denied - Failed to establish: ☐ Eligibility under 8 CFR 274a.12 (a) or (c) ☐ Economic necessity under 8 CFR 274a.12(c)(14), (18) and 8 CFR 214.2(f)	Approved	Denied
			A#	
Subject to the following conditions: ______		☐ Applicant is filing under section 274a.12 ______		

► **START HERE - Type or print in black ink.**

I am applying for:

☒ Permission to accept employment.

☐ Replacement (of lost employment authorization document).

☐ Renewal of my permission to accept employment (attach a copy of your previous employment authorization document).

1. Full Name

Family Name	First Name	Middle Name
[redacted]	[redacted]	[redacted]

2. Other Names Used (include Maiden Name)

Family Name	First Name	Middle Name
[redacted]	[redacted]	

3. U.S. Mailing Address

Street Number and Name	Apt. Number
[redacted]	

Town or City	State	ZIP Code
[redacted]	CA	[redacted]

4. Country of Citizenship or Nationality

Mexico Mexican

5. Place of Birth

Town or City	State/Province	Country
Guadalajara	[redacted]	Mexico

6. Date of Birth (mm/dd/yyyy) 11/20/1989

7. Gender ☒ Male ☐ Female

8. Marital Status

☐ Single ☒ Married ☐ Divorced ☐ Widowed

9.a. Has the Social Security Administration (SSA) ever officially issued a Social Security card to you?

☐ Yes ☒ No

NOTE: If you answered "Yes" to **Item Number 9.a.**, provide the information requested in **Item Number 9.b.**

9.b. Provide your Social Security number (SSN) (if known)

►

10. Do you want the SSA to issue you a Social Security card? (You must also answer "Yes" to **Item Number 11.**, **Consent for Disclosure**, to receive a card.)

☒ Yes ☐ No

NOTE: If you answered "No" to **Item Number 10.**, skip to **Item Number 14.** If you answered "Yes" to **Item Number 10.**, you must also answer "Yes" to **Item Number 11.**

11. Consent for Disclosure: I authorize disclosure of information from this application to the SSA as required for the purpose of assigning me an SSN and issuing me a Social Security card.

☒ Yes ☐ No

NOTE: If you answered "Yes" to **Item Numbers 10. - 11.**, provide the information requested in **Item Numbers 12.a. - 13.b.**

Father's Name

12.a. Family Name (Last Name) [redacted]

Mother's Name (Provide your mother's birth name.)

13.a. Family Name (Last Name) [redacted]

13.b. Given Name (First Name) Maria [redacted]

14. **Alien Registration Number (A-Number) or Form I-94 Number** (if any)

15. **Have you ever before applied for employment authorization from USCIS?**

☐ Yes (Complete the following questions.)

Which USCIS Office? | Dates

Results (Granted or Denied - attach all documentation)

☒ No (Proceed to **Item Number 16.**)

16. **Date of Your Last Arrival or Entry Into the U.S., On or About** (mm/dd/yyyy)

07/16/2011

17. **Place of Your Last Arrival or Entry Into the U.S.**

18. **Status at Last Entry** (B-2 Visitor, F-1 Student, No Lawful Status, etc.)

Unlawful Status

19. **Current Immigration Status** (Visitor, Student, etc.)

Unlawful Status

20. **Eligibility Category.** Go to the **Who May File Form I-765?** section of the Instructions. In the space below, place the letter and number of the eligibility category you selected from the instructions. For example, (a)(8), (c)(17)(iii), etc.

(a)(19)(   )

21. **(c)(3)(C) Eligibility Category.** If you entered the eligibility category (c)(3)(C) in **Item Number 20.** above, list your degree, your employer's name as listed in E-Verify, and your employer's E-Verify Company Identification Number or a valid E-Verify Client Company Identification Number in the space below.

Degree | Employer's Name as listed in E-Verify

Employer's E-Verify Company Identification Number or a Valid E-Verify Client Company Identification Number

22. **(c)(26) Eligibility Category.** If you entered the eligibility category (c)(26) in **Item Number 20.** above, please provide the receipt number of your H-1B principal spouse's most recent Form I-797 Notice of Approval for Form I-129.

23. **(c)(35) and (c)(36) Eligibility Category**

a. If you entered the eligibility category (c)(35) or (c)(36) in **Item Number 20.** above, please provide the receipt number of the Form I-140 beneficiary's Form I-797 Notice of Approval for Form I-140.

b. Have you **EVER** been arrested for and/or convicted of any crime? ☒ Yes ☐ No

NOTE: If you answered "Yes" to **Item Number 23.b.**, refer to **Item Number 5.**, **Item H.** or **Item I.** in the **Who May File Form I-765** section of these Instructions for information about providing court dispositions.

Certification

I certify, under penalty of perjury, that the foregoing is true and correct. Furthermore, I authorize the release of any information that U.S. Citizenship and Immigration Services needs to determine eligibility for the benefit I am seeking. I have read the **Who May File Form I-765** section of the Instructions and have identified the appropriate eligibility category in **Item Number 20.**

Applicant's Signature

Date of Signature (mm/dd/yyyy)

Telephone Number

Signature of Person Preparing Form, If Other Than Applicant

I declare that this document was prepared by me at the request of the applicant and is based on all information of which I have any knowledge.

Preparer's Signature

Date of Signature (mm/dd/yyyy)

Printed Name

Brian D. Lerner

Address

Law Offices of Brian D. Lerner, APC
3233 E. Broadway
Long Beach, CA 90803

Petition for U Nonimmigrant Status
Department of Homeland Security
U.S. Citizenship and Immigration Services

USCIS
Form I-918
OMB No. 1615-0104
Expires 02/28/2019

For USCIS Use Only	Remarks		Receipt	Action Block
	U.S. Embassy Consulate	Validity Dates (mm/dd/yyyy) From: / / To: / /	Wait Listed Stamp Number Date (mm/dd/yyyy)	

To be completed by an attorney or accredited representative (if any).	☒ Select this box if Form G-28 is attached.	Attorney State Bar Number (if applicable)	Attorney or Accredited Representative USCIS Online Account Number (if any)

▶ **START HERE - Type or print in black or blue ink.**

Part 1. Information About You (Person filing this petition as a victim)

1.a. Family Name (Last Name) [redacted]
1.b. Given Name (First Name) [redacted]
1.c. Middle Name [redacted]

Other Names Used (Include maiden name, nicknames, and aliases, if applicable)

2.a. Family Name (Last Name) [redacted]
2.b. Given Name (First Name) [redacted]
2.c. Middle Name

Home Address

3.a. Street Number and Name [redacted]
3.b. ☐ Apt. ☐ Ste. ☐ Flr.
3.c. City or Town [redacted]
3.d. State CA **3.e.** ZIP Code 94066
3.f. Province
3.g. Postal Code
3.h. Country
USA

Safe Mailing Address (if other than Home Address)

4.a. In Care Of Name
4.b. Street Number and Name
4.c. ☐ Apt. ☐ Ste. ☐ Flr.
4.d. City or Town
4.e. State **4.f.** ZIP Code
4.g. Province
4.h. Postal Code
4.i. Country

Other Information

5. Alien Registration Number (A-Number) (if any)
▶ A- [redacted]

6. U.S. Social Security Number (if any)
▶

7. USCIS Online Account Number (if any)
▶

8. Marital Status
☐ Single ☒ Married ☐ Divorced ☐ Widowed

Part 1. Information About You (continued)

9. Gender [X] Male [ ] Female

10. Date of Birth (mm/dd/yyyy) 11/20/1989

11. Country of Birth
Mexico

12. Country of Citizenship or Nationality
Mexico

13. Form I-94 Arrival-Departure Record Number
▶

14. Passport Number [redacted]

15. Travel Document Number

16. Country of Issuance for Passport or Travel Document
Mexico

17. Date of Issuance for Passport or Travel Document (mm/dd/yyyy) 04/02/2016

18. Expiration Date for Passport or Travel Document (mm/dd/yyyy) 04/02/2022

Place and Date of Last Entry into the United States and Date Authorized Stay Expired

19.a. City or Town Otay Mesa

19.b. State CA

20. Date of Last Entry into the United States (mm/dd/yyyy) 07/16/2011

21. Date Authorized Stay Expired (mm/dd/yyyy)

22. Current Immigration Status
Unlawful Status

Part 2. Additional Information About You

Answering "Yes" to the following questions below requires explanations and supporting documentation. Attach relevant documents in support of your claims that you are a victim of criminal activity listed in the Immigration and Nationality Act (INA) section 101(a)(15)(U)(iii). You must also attach a personal narrative statement describing the criminal activity of which you are a victim. If you are only petitioning for U derivative status for qualifying family members subsequent to your (the principal petitioner) initial filing, you are not required to submit evidence supporting the original petition with the new

If you need extra space to complete **Part 2.**, use the space provided in **Part 8. Additional Information**.

Select "Yes" or "No," as appropriate, for each of the following questions.

1. I am a victim of criminal activity listed in the INA at section 101(a)(15)(U)(iii). [X] Yes [ ] No

2. I have suffered substantial physical or mental abuse as a result of having been a victim of this criminal activity. [X] Yes [ ] No

3. I possess information concerning the criminal activity of which I was a victim. [X] Yes [ ] No

4. I am submitting Form I-918, Supplement B, U Nonimmigrant Status Certification, from a certifying official. [X] Yes [ ] No

5. The crime of which I am a victim occurred in the United States (including Indian country and military installations) or violated the laws of the United States. [X] Yes [ ] No

6. I am under 16 years of age. [ ] Yes [X] No

7.a. I was or am in immigration proceedings. [X] Yes [ ] No

If you answered "Yes," select the type of proceedings. If you were in proceedings in the past and are no longer in proceedings, provide the date of action. If you are currently in proceedings, type or print "Current" in the appropriate date field. Select **all applicable** boxes. Use the space provided in **Part 8. Additional Information** to provide an explanation.

7.b. [X] Removal Proceedings
Removal Date (mm/dd/yyyy) 01/03/2011

7.c. [ ] Exclusion Proceedings
Exclusion Date (mm/dd/yyyy)

7.d. [ ] Deportation Proceedings
Deportation Date (mm/dd/yyyy)

7.e. [ ] Rescission Proceedings
Rescission Date (mm/dd/yyyy)

7.f. [ ] Judicial Proceedings
Judicial Date (mm/dd/yyyy)

Part 2. Additional Information About You (continued)

Provide the date of entry, place of entry, and status under which you entered the United States for each entry during the five years preceding the filing of this petition.

8.a. Date of Entry (mm/dd/yyyy)

Place of Entry into the United States

8.b. City or Town

8.c. State

8.d. Status at the Time of Entry (for example, F-1 student, B-2 tourist, entered without inspection)

9.a. Date of Entry (mm/dd/yyyy)

Place of Entry into the United States

9.b. City or Town

9.c. State

9.d. Status at the Time of Entry (for example, F-1 student, B-2 tourist, entered without inspection)

10.a. Date of Entry (mm/dd/yyyy)

Place of Entry into the United States

10.b. City or Town

10.c. State

10.d. Status at the Time of Entry (for example, F-1 student, B-2 tourist, entered without inspection)

If you are outside of the United States, provide the U.S. Consulate or inspection facility or a safe foreign mailing address you want notified if this petition is approved.

11.a. Type of Office (Select **only** one box):

☐ U.S. Consulate ☐ Pre-Flight Inspection

☐ Port-of-Entry

11.b. City or Town

11.c. State

11.d. Country

Safe Foreign Address Where You Want Notification Sent (if other than U.S. Consulate, Pre-Flight Inspection, or Port-of-Entry)

12.a. Street Number and Name

12.b. ☐ Apt. ☐ Ste. ☐ Flr.

12.c. City or Town

12.d. Province

12.e. Postal Code

12.f. Country

Part 3. Processing Information

Answer the following questions about yourself. For the purposes of this petition, you must answer "Yes" to the following questions, if applicable, even if your records were sealed or otherwise cleared or if anyone, including a judge, law enforcement officer, or attorney, told you that you no longer have a record.

NOTE: If you answer "Yes" to **ANY** question in **Part 3.**, provide an explanation in the space provided in **Part 8. Additional Information.**

NOTE: Answering "Yes" does not necessarily mean that U.S. Citizenship and Immigration Services (USCIS) will deny your Petition for U Nonimmigrant Status.

Have you **EVER**:

1.a. Committed a crime or offense for which you have not been arrested? ☐ Yes ☒ No

1.b. Been arrested, cited, or detained by any law enforcement officer (including Department of Homeland Security (DHS), former Immigration and Naturalization Service (INS), and military officers) for any reason? ☒ Yes ☐ No

1.c. Been charged with committing any crime or offense? ☒ Yes ☐ No

1.d. Been convicted of a crime or offense (even if the violation was subsequently expunged or pardoned)? ☒ Yes ☐ No

1.e. Been placed in an alternative sentencing or a rehabilitative program (for example, diversion, deferred prosecution, withheld adjudication, deferred adjudication)? ☐ Yes ☒ No

Part 3. Processing Information (continued)

1.f. Received a suspended sentence, been placed on probation, or been paroled? ☒ Yes ☐ No

1.g. Been in jail or prison? ☒ Yes ☐ No

1.h. Been the beneficiary of a pardon, amnesty, rehabilitation, or other act of clemency or similar action? ☐ Yes ☒ No

1.i. Exercised diplomatic immunity to avoid prosecution for a criminal offense in the United States? ☐ Yes ☒ No

Information About Arrests, Citations, Detentions, or Charges

If you answered "Yes" to any of the above questions, respond to the questions below to provide additional details. If you need extra space, use the space provided in **Part 8. Additional Information**.

2.a Why were you arrested, cited, detained, or charged?

2.b. Date of arrest, citation, detention, or charge (mm/dd/yyyy)

Where were you arrested, cited, detained, or charged?

2.c. City or Town

2.d. State

2.e. Country

2.f. Outcome or disposition (for example, no charges filed, charges dismissed, jail, probation)

3.a Why were you arrested, cited, detained, or charged?

3.b. Date of arrest, citation, detention, or charge (mm/dd/yyyy)

Where were you arrested, cited, detained, or charged?

3.c. City or Town

3.d. State

3.e. Country

3.f. Outcome or disposition (for example, no charges filed, charges dismissed, jail, probation)

Have you **EVER**:

4.a. Engaged in, or do you intend to engage in, prostitution or procurement of prostitution? ☐ Yes ☒ No

4.b. Engaged in any unlawful commercialized vice, including, but not limited to, illegal gambling? ☐ Yes ☒ No

4.c. Knowingly encouraged, induced, assisted, abetted, or aided any alien to try to enter the United States illegally? ☐ Yes ☒ No

4.d. Illicitly trafficked in any controlled substance or knowingly assisted, abetted, or colluded in the illicit trafficking of any controlled substance? ☐ Yes ☒ No

Have you **EVER** committed, planned or prepared, participated in, threatened to, attempted to, conspired to commit, gathered information for, or solicited funds for any of the following:

5.a. Hijacking or sabotage of any conveyance (including an aircraft, vessel, or vehicle)? ☐ Yes ☒ No

5.b. Seizing or detaining, and threatening to kill, injure, or continue to detain, another individual in order to compel a third person (including a governmental organization) to do or abstain from doing any act as an explicit or implicit condition for the release of the individual seized or detained? ☐ Yes ☒ No

5.c. Assassination? ☐ Yes ☒ No

5.d. The use of any firearm with intent to endanger, directly or indirectly, the safety of one or more individuals or to cause substantial damage to property? ☐ Yes ☒ No

5.e. The use of any biological agent, chemical agent, nuclear weapon or device, explosive, or other weapon or dangerous device, with intent to endanger, directly or indirectly, the safety of one or more individuals or to cause substantial damage to property? ☐ Yes ☒ No

Have you **EVER** been a member of, solicited money or members for, provided support for, attended military training (as defined in section 2339D(c)(1) of Title 18, United States Code) by or on behalf of, or been associated with any other group of two or more individuals, whether organized or not, which has been designated as, or has engaged in or has a subgroup which has been designated as, or has engaged in:

6.a. A terrorist organization under section 219 of the INA? ☐ Yes ☒ No

6.b. Hijacking or sabotage of any conveyance (including an aircraft, vessel, or vehicle)? ☐ Yes ☒ No

Part 3. Processing Information (continued)

6.c. Seizing or detaining, and threatening to kill, injure, or continue to detain, another individual in order to compel a third person (including a governmental organization) to do or abstain from doing any act as an explicit or implicit condition for the release of the individual seized or detained? ☐ Yes ☒ No

6.d. Assassination? ☐ Yes ☒ No

6.e. The use of any firearm with intent to endanger, directly or indirectly, the safety of one or more individuals or to cause substantial damage to property? ☒ Yes ☐ No

6.f. The use of any biological agent, chemical agent, nuclear weapon or device, explosive, or other weapon or dangerous device, with intent to endanger, directly or indirectly, the safety of one or more individuals or to cause substantial damage to property? ☐ Yes ☒ No

6.g. Soliciting money or members or otherwise providing material support to a terrorist organization? ☐ Yes ☒ No

Do you intend to engage in the United States in:

7.a. Espionage? ☐ Yes ☒ No

7.b. Any unlawful activity, or any activity the purpose of which is in opposition to, or the control, or overthrow of the government of the United States? ☐ Yes ☒ No

7.c. Solely, principally, or incidentally in any activity related to espionage or sabotage or to violate any law involving the export of goods, technology, or sensitive information? ☐ Yes ☒ No

8. Have you **EVER** been or do you continue to be a member of the Communist or other totalitarian party, except when membership was involuntary? ☐ Yes ☒ No

9. Have you **EVER**, during the period of March 23, 1933 to May 8, 1945, in association with either the Nazi Government of Germany or any organization or government associated or allied with the Nazi Government of Germany, ordered, incited, assisted or otherwise participated in the persecution of any person because of race, religion, nationality, membership in a particular social group, or political opinion? ☐ Yes ☒ No

Have you **EVER** ordered, incited, called for, committed, assisted, helped with, or otherwise participated in any of the following:

10.a. Acts involving torture or genocide? ☐ Yes ☒ No

10.b. Killing any person? ☐ Yes ☒ No

10.c. Intentionally and severely injuring any person? ☐ Yes ☒ No

10.d. Engaging in any kind of sexual conduct or relations with any person who was being forced or threatened? ☐ Yes ☒ No

10.e. Limiting or denying any person's ability to exercise religious beliefs? ☐ Yes ☒ No

10.f. The persecution of any person because of race, religion, national origin, membership in a particular social group, or political opinion? ☐ Yes ☒ No

10.g. Displacing or moving any person from their residence by force, threat of force, compulsion, or duress? ☐ Yes ☒ No

NOTE: If you answered "Yes" to any question in **Item Numbers 10.a. - 10.g.**, please describe the circumstances in **Part 8. Additional Information**.

11. Have you **EVER** advocated that another person commit any of the acts described in the preceding question, urged, or encouraged another person, to commit such acts? ☐ Yes ☒ No

Have you **EVER** been present or nearby when any person was:

12.a. Intentionally killed, tortured, beaten, or injured? ☐ Yes ☒ No

12.b. Displaced or moved from his or her residence by force, compulsion, or duress? ☐ Yes ☒ No

12.c. In any way compelled or forced to engage in any kind of sexual contact or relations? ☐ Yes ☒ No

Have you **EVER**:

13.a. Served in, been a member of, assisted in, or participated in any military unit, paramilitary unit, police unit, self-defense unit, vigilante unit, rebel group, guerilla group, militia, or other insurgent organization? ☐ Yes ☒ No

Part 3. Processing Information (continued)

13.b. Served in any prison, jail, prison camp, detention facility, labor camp, or any other situation that involved detaining persons? ☒ Yes ☐ No

13.c. Served in, been a member of, assisted in, or participated in any group, unit, or organization of any kind in which you or other persons transported, possessed, or used any type of weapon? ☐ Yes ☒ No

NOTE: If you answered "Yes" to any question in **Item Numbers 13.a. - 13.c.**, please describe the circumstances in **Part 8. Additional Information**.

Have you **EVER**:

14.a. Received any type of military, paramilitary, or weapons training? ☐ Yes ☒ No

14.b. Been a member of, assisted in, or participated in any group, unit, or organization of any kind in which you or other persons used any type of weapon against any person or threatened to do so? ☐ Yes ☒ No

14.c. Assisted or participated in selling or providing weapons to any person who to your knowledge used them against another person, or in transporting weapons to any person who to your knowledge used them against another person? ☐ Yes ☒ No

NOTE: If you answered "Yes" to any question in **Item Numbers 14.a. - 14.c.**, please describe the circumstances in **Part 8. Additional Information**.

Have you **EVER**:

15.a. Recruited, enlisted, conscripted, or used any person under 15 years of age to serve in or help an armed force or group? ☐ Yes ☒ No

15.b. Used any person under 15 years of age to take part in hostilities, or to help or provide services to people in combat? ☐ Yes ☒ No

16. Are you **NOW** in removal, exclusion, rescission, or deportation proceedings? ☐ Yes ☒ No

17. Have you **EVER** had removal, exclusion, rescission, or deportation proceedings initiated against you? ☐ Yes ☒ No

18. Have you **EVER** been removed, excluded, or deported from the United States? ☐ Yes ☒ No

19. Have you **EVER** been ordered to be removed, excluded, or deported from the United States? ☒ Yes ☐ No

20. Have you **EVER** been denied a visa or denied admission to the United States? ☒ Yes ☐ No

21. Have you **EVER** been granted voluntary departure by an immigration officer or an immigration judge and failed to depart within the allotted time? ☒ Yes ☐ No

22. Are you **NOW** under a final order or civil penalty for violating section 274C of the INA (producing and/or using false documentation to unlawfully satisfy a requirement of the INA)? ☒ Yes ☐ No

23. Have you **EVER**, by fraud or willful misrepresentation of a material fact, sought to procure or procured a visa or other documentation, for entry into the United States or any immigration benefit? ☒ Yes ☐ No

24. Have you **EVER** left the United States to avoid being drafted into the U.S. Armed Forces or U.S. Coast Guard? ☐ Yes ☒ No

25. Have you **EVER** been a J nonimmigrant exchange visitor who was subject to the 2-year foreign residence requirement and not yet complied with that requirement or obtained a waiver of such? ☐ Yes ☒ No

26. Have you **EVER** detained, retained, or withheld the custody of a child, having a lawful claim to United States citizenship, outside the United States from a United States citizen granted custody? ☐ Yes ☒ No

27. Do you plan to practice polygamy in the United States? ☐ Yes ☒ No

28. Have you **EVER** entered the United States as a stowaway? ☐ Yes ☒ No

29.a. Do you **NOW** have a communicable disease of public health significance? ☐ Yes ☒ No

29.b. Do you **NOW** have or have you **EVER** had a physical or mental disorder and behavior (or a history of behavior that is likely to recur) associated with the disorder which has posed or may pose a threat to the property, safety, or welfare of yourself or others? ☐ Yes ☒ No

29.c. Are you **NOW** or have you **EVER** been a drug abuser or drug addict? ☐ Yes ☒ No

Part 4. Information About Your Spouse and/or Children

If you need extra space to complete **Part 4.**, use the space provided in **Part 8. Additional Information**.

1.a. Family Name (Last Name) [redacted]

1.b. Given Name (First Name) [redacted]

1.c. Middle Name [redacted]

2. Date of Birth (mm/dd/yyyy) 10/13/1993

3. Country of Birth: USA

4. Relationship: Spouse

5. Current Location: USA

6.a. Family Name (Last Name) [redacted]

6.b. Given Name (First Name) [redacted]

6.c. Middle Name [redacted]

7. Date of Birth (mm/dd/yyyy) 03/20/2010

8. Country of Birth: USA

9. Relationship: Child

10. Current Location: USA

11.a. Family Name (Last Name) [redacted]

11.b. Given Name (First Name) [redacted]

11.c. Middle Name [redacted]

12. Date of Birth (mm/dd/yyyy) 03/20/2010

13. Country of Birth: USA

14. Relationship: Child

15. Current Location: USA

16.a. Family Name (Last Name) [redacted]

16.b. Given Name (First Name) [redacted]

16.c. Middle Name [redacted]

17. Date of Birth (mm/dd/yyyy) 03/20/2010

18. Country of Birth: USA

19. Relationship: Child

20. Current Location: USA

21.a. Family Name (Last Name) [redacted]

21.b. Given Name (First Name) [redacted]

21.c. Middle Name [redacted]

22. Date of Birth (mm/dd/yyyy) 05/14/2012

23. Country of Birth: USA

24. Relationship: Child

25. Current Location:

Filing On Behalf of Family Members

26. I am petitioning for one or more qualifying family members. ☐ Yes ☒ No

NOTE: If you answered "Yes" to **Item Number 26.**, you must complete and include Supplement A for each family member for whom you are petitioning.

Part 5. Petitioner's Statement, Contact Information, Declaration, and Signature

NOTE: Read the **Penalties** section of the Form I-918 Instructions before completing this part.

Petitioner's Statement

NOTE: Select the box for either **Item Number 1.a.** or **1.b.** If applicable, select the box for **Item Number 2.**

1.a. [X] I can read and understand English, and I have read and understand every question and instruction on this petition and my answer to every question.

1.b. [ ] The interpreter named in **Part 6.** read to me every question and instruction on this petition and my answer to every question in ______, a language in which I am fluent, and I understood everything.

2. [X] At my request, the preparer named in **Part 7.**, Brian D. Lerner, prepared this petition for me based only upon information I provided or authorized.

Petitioner's Contact Information

3. Petitioner's Daytime Telephone Number

4. Petitioner's Mobile Telephone Number (if any)

5. Petitioner's Email Address (if any)

Petitioner's Declaration and Certification

Copies of any documents I have submitted are exact photocopies of unaltered, original documents, and I understand that USCIS may require that I submit original documents to USCIS at a later date. Furthermore, I authorize the release of any information from any of my records that USCIS may need to determine my eligibility for the immigration benefit I seek.

I further authorize release of information contained in this petition, in supporting documents, and in my USCIS records to other entities and persons where necessary for the administration and enforcement of U.S. immigration laws.

I understand that USCIS may require me to appear for an appointment to take my biometrics (fingerprints, photograph, and/or signature) and, at that time, if I am required to provide biometrics, I will be required to sign an oath reaffirming that:

1) I provided or authorized all of the information contained in, and submitted with, my petition;
2) I reviewed and understood all of the information in, and submitted with, my petition; and
3) All of this information was complete, true, and correct at the time of filing.

I certify, under penalty of perjury, that all of the information in my petition and any document submitted with it were provided or authorized by me, that I reviewed and understand all of the information contained in, and submitted with, my petition, and that all of this information is complete, true, and correct.

Petitioner's Signature

6.a. Petitioner's Signature

➡

6.b. Date of Signature (mm/dd/yyyy)

NOTE TO ALL PETITIONERS: If you do not completely fill out this petition or fail to submit required documents listed in the Instructions, USCIS may deny your petition.

NOTE: A parent or legal guardian may sign for a person who is less than 14 years of age. A legal guardian may sign for a mentally incompetent person.

Part 6. Interpreter's Contact Information, Certification, and Signature

Provide the following information about the interpreter.

Interpreter's Full Name

1.a. Interpreter's Family Name (Last Name)

1.b. Interpreter's Given Name (First Name)

2. Interpreter's Business or Organization Name (if any)

Part 6. Interpreter's Contact Information, Certification, and Signature (continued)

Interpreter's Mailing Address

3.a. Street Number and Name

3.b. ☐ Apt. ☐ Ste. ☐ Flr.

3.c. City or Town

3.d. State 3.e. ZIP Code

3.f. Province

3.g. Postal Code

3.h. Country

Interpreter's Contact Information

4. Interpreter's Daytime Telephone Number

5. Interpreter's Mobile Telephone Number (if any)

6. Interpreter's Email Address (if any)

Interpreter's Certification

I certify, under penalty of perjury, that:

I am fluent in English and ______,

which is the same language specified in **Part 5., Item Number 1.b.**, and I have read to this petitioner in the identified language every question and instruction on this petition and his or her answer to every question. The petitioner informed me that he or she understands every instruction, question, and answer on the petition, including the **Petitioner's Declaration and Certification**, and has verified the accuracy of every answer.

Interpreter's Signature

7.a. Interpreter's Signature

7.b. Date of Signature (mm/dd/yyyy)

Part 7. Contact Information, Declaration, and Signature of the Person Preparing this Petition, if Other Than the Petitioner

Provide the following information about the preparer.

Preparer's Full Name

1.a. Preparer's Family Name (Last Name)
Lerner

1.b. Preparer's Given Name (First Name)
Brian

2. Preparer's Business or Organization Name (if any)
Law Offices of Brian D. Lerner, APC

Preparer's Mailing Address

3.a. Street Number and Name: 3233 E. Broadway

3.b. ☐ Apt. ☐ Ste. ☐ Flr.

3.c. City or Town: Long Beach

3.d. State: CA 3.e. ZIP Code: 90803

3.f. Province

3.g. Postal Code

3.h. Country
UNITED STATES OF AMERICA

Preparer's Contact Information

4. Preparer's Daytime Telephone Number
(562) 495-0554

5. Preparer's Mobile Telephone Number (if any)

6. Preparer's Email Address (if any)
blerner@californiaimmigration.us

Preparer's Statement

7.a. ☐ I am not an attorney or accredited representative but have prepared this petition on behalf of the petitioner and with the petitioner's consent.

7.b. ☐ I am an attorney or accredited representative and my representation of the petitioner in this case ☐ extends ☐ does not extend beyond the preparation of this petition.

NOTE: If you are an attorney or accredited representative whose representation extends beyond preparation of this petition, you may be obliged to submit a completed Form G-28, Notice of Entry of Appearance as Attorney or Accredited Representative, with this petition.

Preparer's Certification

By my signature, I certify, under penalty of perjury, that I prepared this petition at the request of the petitioner. The petitioner then reviewed this completed petition and informed me that he or she understands all of the information contained in, and submitted with, his or her petition, including the **Petitioner's Declaration and Certification**, and that all of this information is complete, true, and correct. I completed this petition based only on information that the petitioner provided to me or authorized me to obtain or use.

Preparer's Signature

8.a. Preparer's Signature

8.b. Date of Signature (mm/dd/yyyy)

Part 8. Additional Information

If you need extra space to provide any additional information within this petition, use the space below. If you need more space than what is provided, you may make copies of this page to complete and file with this petition or attach a separate sheet of paper. Include your name and A-Number (if any) at the top of each sheet; indicate the **Page Number**, **Part Number**, and **Item Number** to which your answer refers; and sign and date each sheet.

1.a. Family Name (Last Name) [redacted]

1.b. Given Name (First Name) [redacted]

1.c. Middle Name [redacted]

2. A-Number (if any) ▶ A- [redacted]

3.a. Page Number: 1 3.b. Part Number: 1 3.c. Item Number: 2a-2c

3.d. OTHER NAMES USED BY [redacted]

4.a. Page Number: 2 4.b. Part Number: 1 4.c. Item Number: 7b

4.d. I tried to enter the United States on July 7, 2011 with a fraudulent green card. I was caught by the border patrol and returned to Mexico on the same day.

5.a. Page Number: 3 5.b. Part Number: 2 5.c. Item Number: 1b-1d

5.d. DESCRIPTION OF CRIMINAL ACTIVITY OF APPLICANT

1) On or about 10/11/2010, I willfully and unlawfully commit an assault upon Edgar PENALOZA with a deadly weapon

2) On or about 10/11/2010, Jose Luis RODRIGUEZ and I willfully, unlawfully, and maliciously defaced, damaged or or destroyed the property of another.

6.a. Page Number: 4 6.b. Part Number: 3 6.c. Item Number: 1g

6.d. JAIL OR PRISON TIME

On the Assault with a deadly weapon charge I was sentenced to 3 years in prison. I actually served 3 months in jail and completed 3 years of probation.

On October 13, 2010, I was arrested and put on an immigration hold and spent some time at the Redwood City county jail and then transferred to U.S. Citizen and Immigration Services. I signed a voluntary departure and and left the United States on January 3, 2011

7.a. Page Number: 7.b. Part Number: 7.c. Item Number:

7.d.

Addendum

Form: I-918, A# 200551380 (Page 1)

Part 4 1&2: Additional information about spouse and/or children.

Family Name:
Relationship: Child
Given Name: Odalis
Middle Name: Zaylee
Date of Birth: 07/27/2016
Country of Birth: USA
Current Location:

Supplement B, U Nonimmigrant Status Certification

Department of Homeland Security
U.S. Citizenship and Immigration Services

USCIS
Form I-918
OMB No. 1615-0104
Expires 02/28/2019

8292

For USCIS Use Only

Remarks

▶ START HERE - Type or print in black or blue ink.

Part 1. Victim Information

1. Alien Registration Number (A-Number) (if any) ▶ A-

2.a. Family Name (Last Name)

2.b. Given Name (First Name)

2.c. Middle Name

Other Names Used (Include maiden names, nicknames, and aliases, if applicable.)

If you need extra space to provide additional names, use the space provided in **Part 7. Additional Information.**

3.a. Family Name (Last Name)

3.b. Given Name (First Name)

3.c. Middle Name

4. Date of Birth (mm/dd/yyyy) 11/20/1989

5. Gend ☒ Ma ☐ Femal

Part 2. Agency Information

1. Name of Certifying Agency

Oakland Police Department-Robbery/Burglary

Name of Certifying Official

2.a. Family Name (Last Name)

2.b. Given Name (First Name)

2.c. Middle Name P

3. Title and Division/Office of Certifying Official

Lieutenant of Police/~~Robbery and Burglar~~ SVS

Name of Head of Certifying Agency

4.a. Family Name (Last Name)

4.b. Given Name (First Name)

4.c. Middle Name E

Agency Address

5.a. Street Number and Name

5.b. ☐ Apt. ☐ Ste. ☐ Flr.

5.c. City or Town Oakland

5.d. State CA 5.f. ZIP Code

5.g. Province

5.h. Postal Code

5.i. Country USA

Other Agency Information

6. Agency Type

☐ Federal ☒ State ☐ Local

7. Case Status

☒ On-going ☐ Completed

☐ Other

8. Certifying Agency Category

☐ Judge ☒ Law Enforcement ☐ Prosecutor

☐ Other

9. Case Number 18-004869

10. FBI Number or SID Number (if applicable)

Part 4. Helpfulness Of The Victim

For the following questions, if the victim is under 16 years of age, incompetent or incapacitated, then a parent, guardian, or next friend may act on behalf of the victim.

1. Does the victim possess information concerning the criminal activity listed in **Part 3.**? ☒ Yes ☐ No

2. Has the victim been helpful, is the victim being helpful, or is the victim likely to be helpful in the investigation or prosecution of the criminal activity detailed above? ☒ Yes ☐ No

3. Since the initiation of cooperation, has the victim refused or failed to provide assistance reasonably requested in the investigation or prosecution of the criminal activity detailed above? ☐ Yes ☒ No

   If you answer "Yes" to **Item Numbers 1. - 3.**, provide an explanation in the space below. If you need extra space to complete this section, use the space provided in **Part 7. Additional Information.**

   The Applicant has continuously cooperated with Lt. ROSIN of the Oakland Police Robbery/Robbery division in the apprehension of the 2 persons who committed this crime. The applicant has also been available at any time to provide any details concerning this criminal act that the Oakland Police may need.

   PLEASE SEE ATTACHED DECLARATION

4. Other. Include any additional information you would like to provide.

   PLEASE SEE ATTACHED DECLARATION

Part 5. Family Members Culpable In Criminal Activity

1. Are any of the victim's family members culpable or believed to be culpable in the criminal activity of which the petitioner is a victim? ☐ Yes ☒ No

If you answered "Yes," list the family members and their criminal involvement. (If you need extra space to complete this section, use the space provided in **Part 7. Additional Information**.)

2.a. Family Name (Last Name)

2.b. Given Name (First Name)

2.c. Middle Name

2.d. Relationship

2.e. Involvement

3.a. Family Name (Last Name)

3.b. Given Name (First Name)

3.c. Middle Name

3.d. Relationship

3.e. Involvement

4.a. Family Name (Last Name)

4.b. Given Name (First Name)

4.c. Middle Name

4.d. Relationship

4.e. Involvement

Part 6. Certification

I am the head of the agency listed in **Part 2.** or I am the person in the agency who was specifically designated by the head of the agency to issue a U Nonimmigrant Status Certification on behalf of the agency. Based upon investigation of the facts, I certify, under penalty of perjury, that the individual identified in **Part 1.** is or was a victim of one or more of the crimes listed in **Part 3.** I certify that the above information is complete, true, and correct to the best of my knowledge, and that I have made and will make no promises regarding the above victim's ability to obtain a visa from U.S. Citizenship and Immigration Services (USCIS), based upon this certification. I further certify that if the victim unreasonably refuses to assist in the investigation or prosecution of the qualifying criminal activity of which he or she is a victim, I will notify USCIS.

1. Signature of Certifying Official (sign in ink)

2. Date of Signature (mm/dd/yyyy) 05/10/2018

3. Daytime Telephone Number

4. Fax Number

Part 7. Additional Information

If you need extra space to complete any item within this supplement, use the space below or attach a separate sheet of paper; type or print the agency's name, petitioner's name, and the Alien Registration Number (A-Number) (if any) at the top of each sheet; indicate the **Page Number, Part Number**, and **Item Number** to which your answer refers; and sign and date each sheet. If you need more space than what is provided, you may also make copies of this page to complete and file with this supplement.

1. Agency Name (

Petitioner's Name

2.a. Family Name (Last Name) [redacted]

2.b. Given Name (First Name) [redacted]

2.c. Middle Name [redacted]

3. A-Number (if any) ► A- [redacted]

4.a. Page Number 1 4.b. Part Number 1 4.c. Item Number 3a-5

4.d. **OTHER NAMES USED BY THE APPLICANT**

1)
2)
3)
4)
5)

5.a. Page Number 5.b. Part Number 5.c. Item Number

5.d.

6.a. Page Number 6.b. Part Number 6.c. Item Number

6.d.

25. I hope and pray that you carefully consider the waiver and grant it so I can move forward with my own conditions as well as moving on with my family.

Date: ____________________ Declarant: ____________________

EXHIBITS

Exhibit '1'

Passport of the Applicant

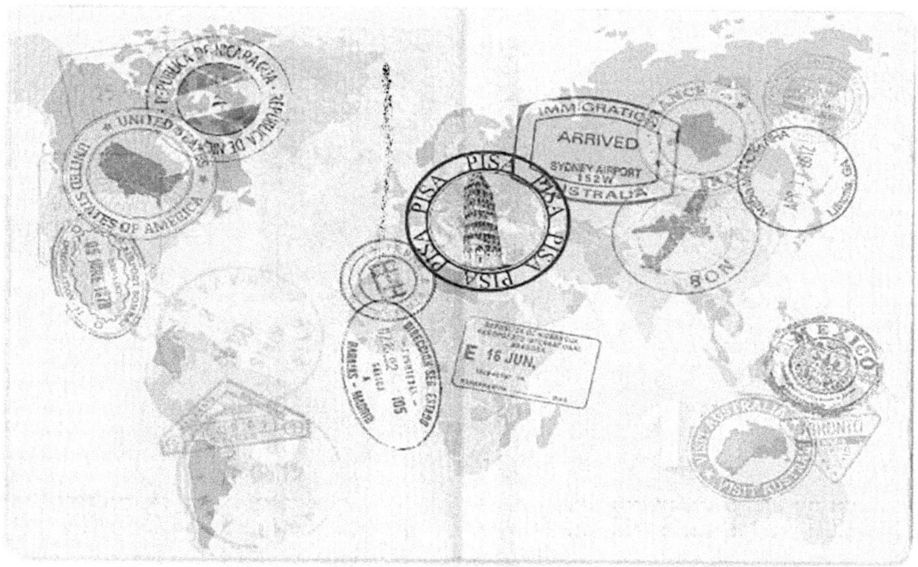

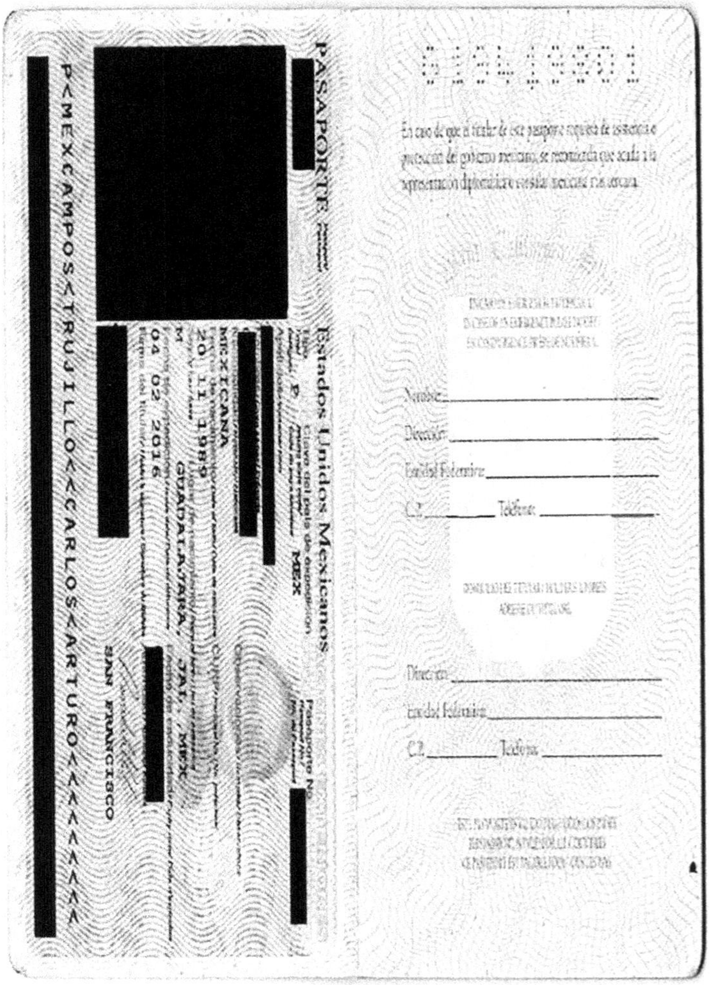
PASAPORTE
Estados Unidos Mexicanos
MEX
MEXICANA
GUADALAJARA, JAL, MEX
SAN FRANCISCO
Nombre:
Dirección:
Entidad Federativa:
C.P.
Teléfono:

Exhibit '2'

Voter's Registration Card and Mexican Consular Identification Card of the Applicant

INSTITUTO FEDERAL ELECTORAL
REGISTRO FEDERAL DE ELECTORES
CREDENCIAL PARA VOTAR
NOMBRE
EDAD 21
SEXO H
DOMICILIO
C ORQUIDEA 6361 A
COL AGRICOLA 45236
ZAPOPAN JAL
CURP CATC891120HJCMRR05
ESTADO 14 MUNICIPIO 120
LOCALIDAD 0001 SECCION 3208
EMISION 2011 VIGENCIA HASTA 2021

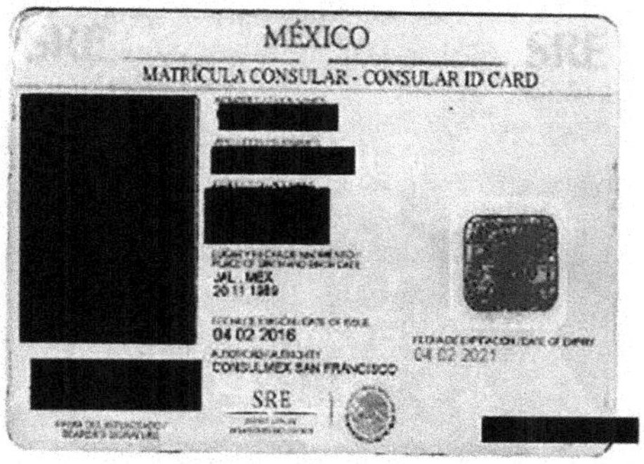
MÉXICO
MATRÍCULA CONSULAR - CONSULAR ID CARD
JAL., MEX
20 11 1989
04 02 2016
CONSULMEX SAN FRANCISCO
04 02 2021
SRE

Exhibit '3'

Copy of the Applicant's Birth Certificate with English Translation

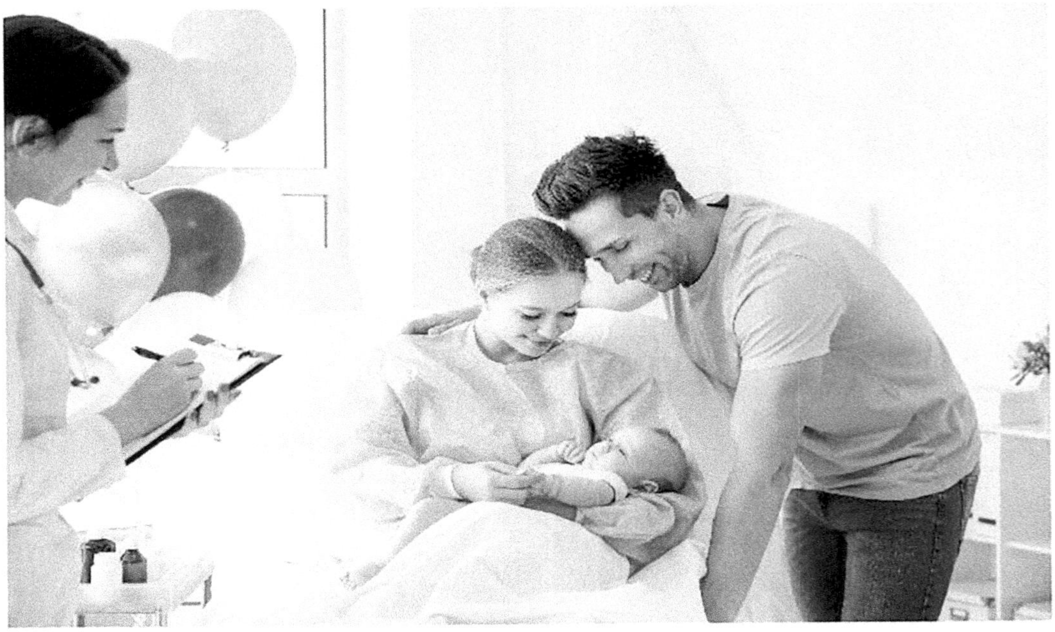

ESTADOS UNIDOS MEXICANOS

FOLIO : 39630

ESTADO LIBRE Y SOBERANO DE JALISCO

REGISTRO CIVIL DE ZAPOPAN

EL(a) C. LIC. HERLINDA LAILA ABDALA CAMPOS OFICIAL DEL REGISTRO CIVIL CON FUNDAMENTO EN EL ART. 21 FRACCION II DE LA LEY DEL REGISTRO CIVIL DEL ESTADO, CERTIFICA Y HACE CONSTAR QUE LA PRESENTE ES COPIA FIEL DEL ACTA DE

NACIMIENTO No. 1776 DEL LIBRO DUPLICADO No. 9

CORRESPONDIENTE AL AÑO 1989 DE LA OFICINA No. 2 DEL MUNICIPIO DE ZAPOPAN JALISCO.

CURP CATC891120HJCMRR05

141200289017766

No. 046493

No. DE CONTROL

ESTADOS UNIDOS MEXICANOS

ESTADO DE JALISCO

REGISTRO CIVIL

ACTA DE NACIMIENTO

ACTA ORIGINAL

CLAVE ÚNICA DEL REG. DE POBLACIÓN

OFICIALIA No. 02 | LIBRO No. 09 | ACTA No. 1776 | LOCALIDAD O DELEGACIÓN PLAZA DEL SOL | FECHA DE REGISTRO DIA 20 MES 12 AÑO 89

MUNICIPIO | ENTIDAD FEDERATIVA

REGISTRADO

SEXO: MASCULINO (X) FEMENINO ( )

NOMBRE

FECHA DE NACIMIENTO 20, veinte de noviembre de 1989, mil novecientos ochenta y nueve HORA 8:45

LUGAR DE NACIMIENTO Guadalajara, Guadalajara, Jalisco

FUE REGISTRADO: VIVO (X) MUERTO ( ) No. DE CERTIFICADO DE NACIMIENTO = = = = =

COMPARECIO: EL PADRE ( ) LA MADRE (X) AMBOS ( ) PERSONA DISTINTA ( )

PADRES

NOMBRE DEL PADRE NACIONALIDAD Mexicana EDAD 19 AÑOS

DOMICILIO Orquidea 116, Agricola, Zapopan, Jalisco

NOMBRE DE LA MADRE NACIONALIDAD Mexicana EDAD 219 AÑOS

DOMICILIO en el antes citado

ABUELOS

ABUELO PATERNO NACIONALIDAD Mexicana

ABUELA PATERNA NACIONALIDAD Mexicana

DOMICILIO(S) en el mismo que los comparecientes

ABUELO MATERNO NACIONALIDAD Mexicana

ABUELA MATERNA NACIONALIDAD Mexicana

DOMICILIO(S) en el mismo que los comparecientes

TESTIGOS

NOMBRE NACIONALIDAD Mexicana EDAD 28 AÑOS

DOMICILIO Mariano Otero 2211, La Calma, Zapopan, Jalisco

NOMBRE NACIONALIDAD Mexicana EDAD 27 AÑOS

DOMICILIO Carnero 5224, Arboledas Arboledas, Zapopan, Jalisco

PERSONA DISTINTA DE LOS PADRES QUE PRESENTA AL REGISTRADO

NOMBRE = = = = = = = = = = = = = = = = = = = PARENTESCO = = = = = = = EDAD = = AÑOS

DOMICILIO =

FIRMAS DE LOS PADRES O DE LA PERSONA DISTINTA QUE PRESENTA AL REGISTRADO

FIRMAS DE LOS TESTIGOS

HUELLA DIGITAL DEL REGISTRADO

SE DIO LECTURA A LA PRESENTE ACTA Y CONFORMES CON SU CONTENIDO LA RATIFICAN Y FIRMAN QUIENES EN ELLA INTERVINIERON Y SABEN HACERLO Y QUIENES NO IMPRIMEN SU HUELLA DIGITAL. DOY FE.

EL C. OFICIAL 02 DEL REGISTRO CIVIL

C. HILDA MARTHA RAMOS RUIZ.

***** English Extract of Spanish Birth Certificate*****
Civil Registration

Name of Registered Child:	[redacted]
Sex:	Male
Date of Birth:	11/20/1989
Place of Birth:	Guadalajara, Guadalajara, Jalisco
Father of Child:	[redacted]
Nationality:	Mexican
Age:	19
Mother of Child:	[redacted]
Nationality:	Mexican
Age	19

*****Certificate Information*****

Issue Date:	12/20/1989
Place of Issue:	[redacted]
Magistrate:	C. Hilda Martha Ramos Ruiz
Record Location:	Plaza Del Sol
Certificate:	1776
Folio:	02
Book:	09

Translator's Certificate of Competence

I, / that the above is an accurate translation of the original Birth Certificate in Spanish and that I am competent in both English and Spanish to render such translation.

06·06·2018
Date

Law Offices of Brian D. Lerner
3233 East Broadway
Long Beach, CA 90803
Tel: (562) 495-0554

Exhibit '4'

Copy of the Birth Certificate of the Applicant's Spouse and Children

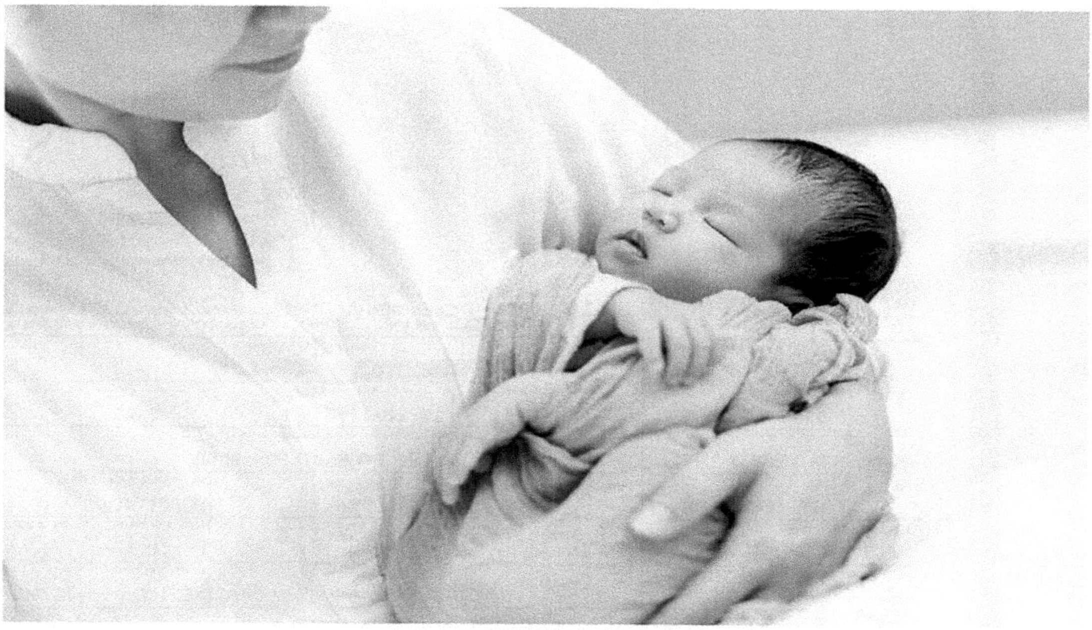

STATE OF CALIFORNIA

CERTIFICATION OF VITAL RECORD

STATE OF CALIFORNIA

DEPARTMENT OF PUBLIC HEALTH

104- [redacted]

STATE FILE NUMBER

CERTIFICATE OF LIVE BIRTH
STATE OF CALIFORNIA
USE BLACK INK ONLY

LOCAL REGISTRATION DISTRICT AND CERTIFICATE NUMBER

THIS CHILD	1A. NAME OF CHILD—FIRST (GIVEN): CRISTAL	1B. MIDDLE: [redacted]	1C. LAST (FAMILY): [redacted]		
	2. SEX: FEMALE	3A. THIS BIRTH SINGLE, TWIN, ETC.: SINGLE	3B. IF MULTIPLE, THIS CHILD 1ST, 2ND, ETC.: -	4A. DATE OF BIRTH: 10/13/1993	4B. HOUR: 0247
PLACE OF BIRTH	5A. PLACE OF BIRTH—NAME OF HOSPITAL OR FACILITY: NORTHBAY MEDICAL CENTER	5B. STREET ADDRESS: 1200 B. GALE WILSON BLVD.			
	5C. CITY: FAIRFIELD	5D. COUNTY: [redacted]	5E. PLANNED PLACE OF BIRTH: HOSPITAL		
FATHER OF CHILD	6A. NAME OF FATHER—FIRST (GIVEN): [redacted]	6B. MIDDLE: -	6C. LAST (FAMILY): [redacted]	7. STATE OF BIRTH: MEXICO	8. DATE OF BIRTH: 11/9/64
MOTHER OF CHILD	9A. NAME OF MOTHER—FIRST (GIVEN): VIRGINIA	9B. MIDDLE: -	9C. LAST (MAIDEN): GUTIERREZ	10. STATE OF BIRTH: MEXICO	11. DATE OF BIRTH: 1/5/67
PARENT'S CERTIFICATION	I certify that I have reviewed the stated information and that it is true and correct to the best of my knowledge	12A. PARENT OR OTHER INFORMANT—SIGNATURE: [redacted]		12B. RELATIONSHIP TO CHILD: PARENT (S)	12C. DATE SIGNED: 10/13/93
CERTIFICATION OF BIRTH	I certify that the child was born alive at the date, hour and place stated	13A. ATTENDANT'S OR CERTIFIER'S SIGNATURE—DEGREE OR TITLE: [redacted]		13B. LICENSE NUMBER: NMW 967	13C. DATE SIGNED: 10/19/93
	13D. TYPED NAME, TITLE AND MAILING ADDRESS OF ATTENDANT: MARTHA BARBATO, CNM, 1200 B GALE WILSON BLVD, FF			14. TYPED NAME AND TITLE OF CERTIFIER IF OTHER THAN ATTENDANT	
LOCAL REGISTRAR	15A. DATE OF DEATH	15B. STATE FILE NO.	16. LOCAL REGISTRAR—SIGNATURE: [signature]		17. DATE ACCEPTED FOR REGISTRATION: OCT 2 8 1993

This is to certify that this document is a true copy of the official record filed with Vital Records.

DATE ISSUED

JAMES GREENE MD MS

DEC -7 2015

0041563 37

STATE OF CALIFORNIA
CERTIFICATION OF VITAL RECORD

COUNTY OF SAN MATEO

HEALTH SYSTEM

SAN MATEO, CALIFORNIA

CERTIFICATE OF LIVE BIRTH

STATE OF CALIFORNIA
USE BLACK INK ONLY

STATE FILE NUMBER

1201241002001
LOCAL REGISTRATION NUMBER

THIS CHILD	1A. NAME OF CHILD - FIRST	[redacted]
	1B. MIDDLE	[redacted]
	1C. LAST	[redacted]
	2. SEX	Male
	3A. THIS BIRTH, SINGLE, TWIN, ETC.	Single
	3B. IF MULTIPLE, THIS CHILD 1ST, 2ND, ETC.	-
	4A. DATE OF BIRTH	05/14/2012
	4B. HOUR - 24 HOUR CLOCK TIME	0858
PLACE OF BIRTH	5A. PLACE OF BIRTH - NAME OF HOSPITAL OR FACILITY	Mills-Peninsula Health Services
	5B. STREET ADDRESS - STREET AND NUMBER, OR LOCATION	[redacted]
	5C. CITY	Burlingame
	5D. COUNTY	San Mateo
FATHER/PARENT	6A. NAME OF FATHER/PARENT - FIRST	-
	6B. MIDDLE	-
	6C. LAST	-
MOTHER/PARENT	9A. NAME OF MOTHER/PARENT - FIRST	[redacted]
	9B. MIDDLE	[redacted]
	9C. LAST - BIRTH NAME	[redacted]
	10. BIRTHPLACE - STATE/COUNTRY	CA
	11. DATE OF BIRTH	10/13/1993
INFORMANT AND BIRTH CERTIFICATION	12A. INFORMANT - SIGNATURE	[signature]
	12B. RELATIONSHIP TO CHILD	Mother
	12C. DATE SIGNED	05/15/2012
	13A. ATTENDANT/CERTIFIER - SIGNATURE AND DEGREE OR TITLE	[signature], MD
	13B. LICENSE NUMBER	A60135
	13C. DATE SIGNED	05/15/2012
	13D. TYPED NAME, TITLE AND MAILING ADDRESS OF ATTENDANT	Jacqueline Fletcher, M.D., 1501 Trousdale Drive - 4th floor, Burlingame, CA 94010
LOCAL REGISTRAR	16. LOCAL REGISTRAR - SIGNATURE	SCOTT A. MORROW, M.D.
	17. DATE ACCEPTED FOR REGISTRATION	05/24/2012

CERTIFIED COPY OF VITAL RECORDS

STATE OF CALIFORNIA
COUNTY OF SAN MATEO } SS

DATE ISSUED 06/04/2012

This is a true and exact reproduction of the document officially registered and placed on file in the office of the SAN MATEO COUNTY HEALTH SYSTEM.

STATE OF CALIFORNIA

CERTIFICATION OF VITAL RECORD

COUNTY OF SAN MATEO

HEALTH SYSTEM

SAN MATEO, CALIFORNIA

CERTIFICATE OF LIVE BIRTH

STATE OF CALIFORNIA

USE BLACK INK ONLY

STATE FILE NUMBER

LOCAL REGISTRATION NUMBER: 1201641003129

1A NAME OF CHILD - FIRST	
1B MIDDLE	
1C LAST	
2 SEX	FEMALE
3A THIS BIRTH, SINGLE, TWIN, ETC	SINGLE
3B IF MULTIPLE, THIS CHILD 1ST, 2ND, ETC	-
4A DATE OF BIRTH - MM/DD/CCYY	07/27/2016
4B HOUR - 24 HOUR CLOCK TIME	1540
5A PLACE OF BIRTH - NAME OF HOSPITAL OR FACILITY	MILLS PENINSULA HEALTH SERVICES
5B STREET ADDRESS - STREET AND NUMBER, OR LOCATION	
5C CITY	BURLINGAME
5D COUNTY	SAN MATEO
NAME OF PARENT (FATHER) - BIRTHPLACE STATE/COUNTRY	MEXICO
DATE OF BIRTH	11/20/1989
NAME OF PARENT (MOTHER) - BIRTHPLACE STATE/COUNTRY	CA
DATE OF BIRTH	10/13/1993
I CERTIFY THAT I HAVE REVIEWED THE STATED INFORMATION AND THAT IT IS TRUE AND CORRECT TO THE BEST OF MY KNOWLEDGE — RELATIONSHIP TO CHILD	PARENTS
DATE SIGNED	07/28/2016
I CERTIFY THAT THE CHILD WAS BORN ALIVE AT THE DATE, HOUR AND PLACE STATED — LICENSE NUMBER	A88683
DATE SIGNED	07/28/2016
TYPED NAME, TITLE AND MAILING ADDRESS OF ATTENDANT	ZELDA DE LA CRUZ,MD,1 BAYWOOD AVE #7,SAN MATEO
14 TYPED NAME AND TITLE OF CERTIFIER IF OTHER THAN ATTENDANT	
15A DATE OF DEATH - MM/DD/CCYY	
15B STATE FILE NO. - STATE USE ONLY	
16 LOCAL REGISTRAR - SIGNATURE	SCOTT A. MORROW, M.D.
17 DATE ACCEPTED FOR REGISTRATION - MM/DD/CCYY	08/04/2016

CASANMATO1

CERTIFIED COPY OF VITAL RECORD

STATE OF CALIFORNIA, COUNTY OF SAN MATEO

This is a true and exact reproduction of the document officially registered and placed on file in the office of the SAN MATEO COUNTY HEALTH SYSTEM.

01/10/2017 Jessica Hernandez

000913454

STATE OF CALIFORNIA

CERTIFICATION OF VITAL RECORD

COUNTY OF SAN MATEO

HEALTH SYSTEM

SAN MATEO, CALIFORNIA

CERTIFICATE OF LIVE BIRTH

STATE OF CALIFORNIA

USE BLACK INK ONLY

STATE FILE NUMBER

1201041001150

LOCAL REGISTRATION NUMBER

THIS CHILD	1A. NAME OF CHILD - FIRST	1B. MIDDLE	1C. LAST		
	2. SEX: Male	3A. THIS BIRTH SINGLE, TWIN, ETC.: Single	3B. IF MULTIPLE, THIS CHILD 1ST, 2ND, ETC.: -	4A. DATE OF BIRTH - MM/DD/CCYY: 03/20/2010	4B. HOUR - 24 HOUR CLOCK TIME: 0358
PLACE OF BIRTH	5A. PLACE OF BIRTH - NAME OF HOSPITAL OR FACILITY: Mills-Peninsula Health Services	5B. STREET ADDRESS - STREET AND NUMBER, OR LOCATION			
	5C. CITY: Burlingame	5D. COUNTY: San Mateo			
FATHER/PARENT	6A. NAME OF FATHER/PARENT - FIRST	6B. MIDDLE	6C. LAST	7. BIRTHPLACE - STATE/COUNTRY: MEXICO	8. DATE OF BIRTH - MM/DD/CCYY: 11/20/1989
MOTHER/PARENT	9A. NAME OF MOTHER/PARENT - FIRST	9B. MIDDLE	9C. LAST - BIRTH NAME	10. BIRTHPLACE - STATE/COUNTRY: CA	11. DATE OF BIRTH - MM/DD/CCYY: 10/13/1993
INFORMANT AND BIRTH CERTIFICATION	I CERTIFY THAT I HAVE REVIEWED THE STATED INFORMATION AND THAT IT IS TRUE AND CORRECT TO THE BEST OF MY KNOWLEDGE		12B. RELATIONSHIP TO CHILD: Mother	12C. DATE SIGNED - MM/DD/CCYY: 03/21/2010	
	I CERTIFY THAT THE CHILD WAS BORN ALIVE AT THE DATE, HOUR, AND PLACE STATED	13A. ATTENDANT/CERTIFIER - SIGNATURE AND DEGREE OR TITLE: MD	13B. LICENSE NUMBER: A99819	13C. DATE SIGNED - MM/DD/CCYY: 03/21/2010	
	13D. TYPED NAME, TITLE AND MAILING ADDRESS OF ATTENDANT: Emily Yu, M.D., San Mateo Dr., San Mateo, CA 94401		14. TYPED NAME AND TITLE OF CERTIFIER IF OTHER THAN ATTENDANT		
LOCAL REGISTRAR	15A. DATE OF DEATH - MM/DD/CCYY	15B. STATE FILE NO. - STATE USE ONLY	16. LOCAL REGISTRAR - SIGNATURE: SCOTT A. MORROW, M.D.	17. DATE ACCEPTED FOR REGISTRATION - MM/DD/CCYY: 03/30/2010	

CERTIFIED COPY OF VITAL RECORDS JUN 0 8 2010

STATE OF CALIFORNIA
COUNTY OF SAN MATEO } SS DATE ISSUED

This is a true and exact reproduction of the document officially registered and placed on file in the office of the SAN MATEO COUNTY HEALTH SYSTEM.

GREAT SEAL OF THE STATE OF CALIFORNIA — EUREKA

COUNTY OF SAN MATEO

Exhibit '5'

Copy of the Marriage Certificate of the Applicant and the Applicant's Spouse

State of Nevada

Marriage Certificate

NO. MA2016-7779

DOC 2016307904
12/27/2016 11:09:41 AM
Requested By
WILLIAM K OLDS
Washoe County Recorder
Lawrence R. Burtness - Recorder
Page 1 of 1

State of Nevada }
County of Washoe } ss.

This is to certify that the undersigned, Officiant (Title)

did on the 25th day of December, 2016

at ARCH OF RENO WEDDING CHAPEL, RENO (Address or Church) (City) Nevada,

join in lawful wedlock [redacted]

of SAN BRUNO (City) State/Country of CALIFORNIA

Date of Birth 11/20/1989, and [redacted]

of SAN BRUNO (City) State/Country of CALIFORNIA

Date of Birth 10/13/1993, with their mutual consent, in the presence of [redacted] and

________________, witnesses.

SEAL OF WASHOE COUNTY — STATE OF NEVADA

William K. Olds
Signature of person performing marriage

William K. Olds, Minister
Print name under signature

Officiant
Official title of person performing the marriage

WASHOE COUNTY CLERK

Couple's Mailing Address:

MINISTER OR JUDGE: **YOU** MUST PRESENT THIS **ORIGINAL** DOCUMENT **WITHIN 10 DAYS** TO WASHOE COUNTY RECORDER, P.O. BOX 11130, 1001 E 9TH STREET, RENO, NV 89520-0027

By the raised Washoe County Recorder seal on this page, I certify that this document is a correct copy of the original recorded in my office.

Lawrence R. Burtness
Lawrence R. Burtness, County Recorder, Washoe County, Nevada

DEPUTY RECORDER / DATE
DEC 27 2016

Exhibit '6'

Court Documents of the Applicant from October 21, 2010

AKA. [redacted]

SUPERIOR COURT OF CALIFORNIA, COUNTY OF SAN MATEO

(For Court Use Only)

THE PEOPLE OF THE STATE OF CALIFORNIA — Plaintiff

vs. [redacted] — Defendant

DECLARATION CONCERNING ☐ PLEA OF ☑ CHANGE OF PLEA TO GUILTY OR NOLO CONTENDERE; and FINDING and ORDER

FILED SAN MATEO COUNTY OCT 21 2010 Clerk of the Superior Court By DEPUTY CLERK

Case Number SC - NF397232A

SC072011

FILED SAN MATEO COUNTY OCT 22 2010 BY CLERK OF THE SUPERIOR COURT DEPUTY CLERK

I, the above named defendant in the above-entitled criminal action, and in support of my motion, which will be made in open court personally and by my attorney, ☑ to change my plea(s) to ☐ to plead ☐ guilty ☑ nolo contendere, do declare:

1. My attorney in this action is RAY BUENAVENTURA

2. I am charged in the Complaint in this action with having violated P.C. 245(A)(1), P.C. 594 (B)(1) (code, section(s), count(s)) Count 1 felony, Count felony.

PC = Penal code

3. I desire to ☐ plead ☑ change my plea(s) to NO CONTEST (guilty/nolo contendere) to P.C. 245(A)(1) "by means of force likely to produce great bodily injury" (non-strike) felony (state code, section(s) and count(s), including lesser offense(s) to which plea is to be made)

4. I DO (do/do not) understand the nature of the charge(s) against me.

5. I HAVE (have/have not) discussed the nature of the charge(s) against me and the possible defenses thereto with my attorney.

6. My attorney HAS (has/has not) explained my constitutional rights to a trial by jury, confront witnesses against me, the process of the Court to compel the attendance of witnesses on my behalf, the right to remain silent or, if I so choose, to testify for myself.

7. I DO (do/do not) realize that I give up these rights by pleading guilty or nolo contendere. I understand that a plea of nolo contendere has the same legal effect as a plea of guilty.

8. I understand that if I am not a citizen, conviction of the offense for which I have been charged will have the consequences of deportation, exclusion from admission to the United States or denial of naturalization.

9. My decision to ☑ change my plea(s) to ☐ plead NO CONTEST HAS (guilty/nolo contendere (has/has not)) been made freely and voluntarily, without threat or fear to me or anyone closely related to or associated with me.

10. My attorney HAS (has/has not) explained that the maximum penalty, including penalty assessments, which could be imposed as a result of my plea(s) of guilty or nolo contendere is 4 years prison, 4 years parole, $10,000 fine, $10,000 rest min $200 +10%, genetic marker testing, actual restitution

11. I HAVE NOT (have/have not) been induced to plead guilty or nolo contendere by any promise or representation of a lesser, sentence, probation, reqard, immunity, or anything else except:

3 yr Probation, 120 days CJ, Drivers License suspension during term of probation, Fines $ 200 + 30 + 30 + 200 no Contact w/ Victim waive prob report. No driving while on probation

(NOTE: Any agreement on sentence where state prison is imposed included parole, and where probation is granted may still subject a defendant to the maximum penalty (see #10) if probation is later violated.)

12. I DO (do/do not) waive my right to be sentenced by the judge taking my plea and understand sentencing may occur before another judge.

13. I DO (do/do not) understand that the matter of probation and sentence is to be determined solely by the Court and will not be decided until the report and recommendation by the Probation Department has been considered.

The Court reserves the right to withdraw its consent to any sentence limitation agreement; and, in the event, I will be permitted to withdraw my plea(s) of guilty or nolo contendere and all charges will be reinstated.

EXECUTED in San Mateo County, California on 10-21-10

Sight Translated by Carol M. Palacio X [signature]
(Defendant's Signature)

Ray Buenaventura states that he/she is the above-named defendant's attorney in the above-entitled action; he/she personally read and explained the contents of the above declaration to the defendant; he/she personally observed the defendant fill in, date and sign said declaration; he/she, after having investigated this case and the possible defenses thereto, concurs in the defendant's ples(s) of guilty or nolo contendere to the charge(s) as set forth by the defendant in the above declaration and stipulates there is a factual basis for the plea(s).

DATED: 10-21-10 [signature]
(Attorney's Signature)

The People of the State of California, plaintiff in the above-entitled criminal action, by and through its attorney, concur and stipulate there is a factual basis for the plea(s).

DATED: 10/21/10 JAMES P. FOX, DISTRICT ATTORNEY

By [signature] Sharon Le
Deputy — Assistant District Attorney

FINDINGS AND ORDER

The defendant personally and by his attorney in open court having this date entered a plea of ☐ guilty ☐ nolo contendere, and having been advised as to his/her rights, said plea is hereby accepted and ordered entered. The Court finds that the defendant made a knowing, intelligent and voluntary waiver of the above rights.

DATED: 10/21/10 [signature]
JUDGE

JAMES P FOX
DISTRICT ATTORNEY
SAN MATEO COUNTY
STATE BAR NO. 45169
BY: SEAN F GALLAGHER
DEPUTY DISTRICT ATTORNEY
1050 MISSION RD
SOUTH SAN FRAN, CA 94080

TELEPHONE: (650) 877-5454

ATTORNEYS FOR PLAINTIFF

FILED
SAN MATEO COUNTY
OCT 22 2010
CLERK OF THE SUPERIOR COURT
BY DEPUTY CLERK

FILED
SAN MATEO COUNTY
OCT 15 2010
Clerk of the Superior Court
By DEPUTY CLERK

IN AND FOR THE SUPERIOR COURT OF CALIFORNIA

COUNTY OF SAN MATEO

SC072011
NF397232

THE PEOPLE OF THE STATE OF CALIFORNIA, PLAINTIFF,	) SB CASE) DA CASE: COM 0424685) (FELONY)
V.	) COMPLAINT
* [redacted] AKA AKA AKA AKA AKA AKA * [redacted] DEFENDANT(S).	)

I, THE UNDERSIGNED, SAY, ON INFORMATION AND BELIEF, THAT IN THE COUNTY OF SAN MATEO, STATE OF CALIFORNIA:

1.

COUNT: 001, ON OR ABOUT 10/11/2010, AND DID WILLFULLY AND UNLAWFULLY COMMIT AN ASSAULT UPON WITH A DEADLY WEAPON, TO WIT: VEHICLE, AND/OR BY MEANS OF FORCE LIKELY TO PRODUCE GREAT BODILY INJURY, IN VIOLATION OF PENAL CODE SECTION 245(A)(1), A FELONY.

COUNT: 002, ON OR ABOUT 10/11/2010, AND DID WILLFULLY, UNLAWFULLY AND MALICIOUSLY DEFACE, DAMAGE OR DESTROY THE PROPERTY OF ANOTHER, THE AMOUNT OF DEFACEMENT, DAMAGE OR DESTRUCTION BEING FOUR HUNDRED DOLLARS ($400.00) OR MORE, IN VIOLATION OF PENAL CODE SECTION 594(B)(1), A FELONY. S17 as to Rodriguez

I DECLARE UNDER PENALTY OF PERJURY THAT THE FOREGOING IS TRUE AND CORRECT EXCEPT FOR THOSE THINGS STATED ON INFORMATION AND BELIEF AND THOSE I BELIEVE TO BE TRUE.

EXECUTED ON 10/15/10, AT SOUTH SAN FRANCISCO, CA 94080.

SAH

COMPLAINANT

COUNTY OF SAN MATEO

Office of the Sheriff

GREG MUNKS
SHERIFF

CARLOS G. BOLANOS
UNDERSHERIFF

TRISHA L. SANCHEZ
ASSISTANT SHERIFF

400 COUNTY CENTER • REDWOOD CITY • CALIFORNIA 94063-1662 • TELEPHONE (650) 599-1664 • www.smcsheriff.com

ADDRESS ALL COMMUNICATIONS TO THE SHERIFF

To Whom It May Concern:

Based upon the following form of Identification

- ☐ California Driver's License
- ☐ California ID Card
- ☐ U.S. Passport
- ☑ Other MATRICULA CARD

A thorough search by name only has been conducted on the below listed applicant for criminal record information in San Mateo County:

NAME: [redacted] DOB: 11/20/1989

AKA/S: [redacted]

SHERIFF'S ID #: 1152555

☐ No criminal record with the San Mateo County Sheriff's Office.

☑ Has a criminal record in the County of San Mateo.
Please see attached copy of print out for local criminal record information since 1989. Contact the appropriate court for further disposition information of arrest record on the above applicant.

☐ Has a criminal record in the County of San Mateo.
Any record prior to 1990 is not available from this office. Please contact the appropriate court for further disposition information of arrest record on the above subject.

☐ Arrest records prior to 1990 are purged. No information is available.

Please be advised this search reflects local criminal records only and does not reflect any criminal history outside of San Mateo County.

Greg Munks, Sheriff

By: Date: 02/27/2015

Name: K.STANTON

☑ Criminal Records Technician I/II
☐ Criminal Records Supervisor

SAN MATEO COUNTY SHERIFF OFFICE

Inmate History - Arrest With Charges

Facility: MCF (1)

Inmate: [redacted]

A Name	DOB	Number	Housing	Sex	Race	In	Out	Days
Booking Num	Type / Booking Date / Release Date / Cnt Type Section	Court / Rel Reason / Statute Description	Case Number / Docket Number			Arrest Date / Disposition	Arrest Agncy / Orig Agncy	Bail / Schd Release / Charge Status
[redacted]	11/20/1989	1152555		M	H	10-13-10 23:56	01-04-11 9:16	83

0625908.2
- **Arrest** OPEN CHARGES — SC072011A — 10-13-10 18:26 SB
- **Booking** 10-22-10 13:55 SCRWC — SC072011A — 0.00
- **Release** 01-04-11 09:16 TIME SERVED — Schd01-01-11 00:00

Warrant

Cnt	Type	Section	Statute	Description	Charge Status
1	F	182(A)(1)	PC	CONSPIRE TO COMMIT A CRIME	RELEASE
1	F	245(A)(1)	PC	ASSAULT W/DEADLY WEAPON OTHER THAN FII	RELEASE

0625908.1
- **Arrest** FOREIGN HOLD - IMMIGRATI(— 10-14-10 09:05 IMMIGRATION
- **Booking** 10-14-10 09:06 DATA CONVA — NO BAIL
- **Release** 01-04-11 09:16 LAW ENFORCEMENT RELEASE

Warrant

Cnt	Type	Section	Statute	Description	Charge Status
1	F	TITLE 8	US	TITLE 8	ARREST
1	F	TITLE 8	US	TITLE 8 I.C.E. HOLD	ARREST

0625908
- **Arrest** OPEN CHARGES — NF397232A — 10-13-10 18:26 SB
- **Booking** 10-14-10 00:59 MCSSF — NF397232A — 25000.00
- **Release** 01-04-11 09:16 CASE TRANSFERRED

Warrant

Cnt	Type	Section	Statute	Description	Charge Status
1	F	182(A)(1)	PC	CONSPIRE TO COMMIT A CRIME	RELEASE
1	F	245(A)(1)	PC	ASSAULT W/DEADLY WEAPON OTHER THAN FII	RELEASE

Total Inmates: 1 **Total Bookings:** 3

CRIMINAL

CASE SUMMARY

CASE NO. SC072011A

The People of the State of California
vs.

§ Location: **Criminal**
§ Filed on: **10/21/2010**
§ District Attorney Number: [redacted]
§ DMV Docket Number: [redacted]
§
§

CASE INFORMATION

Offense	Statute	Deg	Date	Case Type: **Complaint**
Jurisdiction: **San Bruno**				
001. PC245(A)(1)-FEL-ASSAULT W/DEADLY WEAPON OTHER THAN FIREARM OR GBI FORCE Charge #: 001 Arrest: 10/13/2010 SBPD - San Bruno Police Department	245(A)(1)	F	10/11/2010	

Related Cases
NF397232A (Certified)

DATE	CASE ASSIGNMENT
	Current Case Assignment Case Number SC072011A Court Criminal Date Assigned 10/21/2010

PARTY INFORMATION

Plaintiff **The People of the State of California**

Defendant [redacted]

DATE	EVENTS & ORDERS OF THE COURT	INDEX
10/21/2010	Information Filed	
10/21/2010	Conversion Event *FD859:* *CERTIFICATION PURSUANT TO 859A FILED.*	
10/21/2010	Conversion Event *HHELD:* *HEARING HELD ON 10 21 10 AT 1:31 P.M. IN SUPERIOR COURT - SOUTH SAN FRANCISCO , D- 5 , HON. MARTA S DIAZ, JUDGE , PRESIDING. CLERK: TAMMY MAGILL , REPORTER: JANICE SCOTT , CLERK2: NONE , DEPUTY D.A. MEGAN WILKINS , DEFENSE COUNSEL PRESENT: BUENAVENTURA .*	
10/21/2010	Conversion Event *FDMIS:* *COMPLAINT FILED.*	
10/21/2010	Conversion Event *HHSEN:* *SENTENCING*	
10/21/2010	Conversion Event *FDCOP:* *DECLARATION RE PLEA CHANGE OF PLEA; FINDING AND ORDER SIGNED IN OPEN COURT.*	

10/21/2010	Conversion Event *APDFA:* *DEFENDANT PRESENT.*
10/21/2010	Conversion Event *APDAD:* *DEPUTY DA MEGAN WILKINS DESIGNATED AS PROSECUTING ATTORNEY OF RECORD.*
10/21/2010	Conversion Event *WRTSE:* *TIME WAIVED FOR SENTENCING.*
10/21/2010	Conversion Event *WREAJ:* *DEFENDANT WAIVED FORMAL ARRAIGNMENT FOR JUDGMENT.*
10/21/2010	Conversion Event *SLSEN:* *DEFENDANT STATED THERE IS NO LEGAL CAUSE WHY SENTENCE SHOULD NOT NOW BE PRONOUNCED.*
10/21/2010	Conversion Event *MICMF:* *THE COURT MAKES THE FOLLOWING FINDINGS AND OR ORDERS:*
10/21/2010	Conversion Event *PRISS:* *IMPOSITION OF SENTENCE IS SUSPENDED.*
10/21/2010	Conversion Event *PRISA:* *DEFENDANT IS ADMITTED TO SUPERVISED PROBATION FOR A PERIOD OF 3 YEAR (S), 0 MONTH(S) UPON THE FOLLOWING TERMS AND CONDITIONS:*
10/21/2010	Conversion Event *FIRFF:* *DEFENDANT SHALL PAY A $200.00 RESTITUTION FUND FINE AS MANDATED BY PENAL CODE SECTION 1202.4 PLUS 10 % OR $0.00 COLLECTION FEE.*
10/21/2010	Conversion Event *FIPAA:* *PAYMENTS TO BE MADE TO PROBATION DEPARTMENT.*
10/21/2010	Conversion Event *SECJT:* *DEFENDANT SHALL SERVE A TOTAL OF 0 DAY(S), 4 MONTH(S), 0 YEAR(S) IN THE COUNTY JAIL.*
10/21/2010	Conversion Event *SETBD:* *CREDIT FOR TIME SERVED TO BE DETERMINED BY SHERIFF'S OFFICE OR PROBATION DEPARTMENT.*
10/21/2010	Conversion Event *SEOBR:* *DEFENDANT TO OBEY ALL RULES AND REGULATIONS OF THE JAIL FACILITY OR INSTITUTION IN WHICH PLACED.*
10/21/2010	Conversion Event *PRCON:*

	CONDITIONS OF PROBATION (IN ADDITION TO THE USUAL CONDITIONS RE: SUPERVISION, EMPLOYMENT, OBEDIENCE OF LAWS, REMAINING IN STATE AND KEEPING PROBATION OFFICER ADVISED OF WHEREABOUTS):
10/21/2010	Conversion Event *PRSAS:* *DEFENDANT SHALL SUBMIT TO SEARCH AND SEIZURE OF HIS HER PERSON, PLACE OF RESIDENCE OR AREA UNDER HIS HER CONTROL, OR VEHICLE, BY ANY PROBATION OFFICER OR PEACE OFFICER, DURING THE DAY OR NIGHT, WITH OR WITHOUT HIS HER CONSENT, WITH OR WITHOUT A SEARCH WARRANT, AND WITHOUT REGARD TO PROBABLE CAUSE.*
10/21/2010	Conversion Event *PRSMC:* *DEFENDANT SHALL SEEK AND MAINTAIN FULL-TIME EMPLOYMENT AND PARTICIPATION IN A VOCATIONAL OR EDUCATIONAL PROGRAM AS DIRECTED BY THE PROBATION OFFICER.*
10/21/2010	Conversion Event *PRRSC:* *DEFENDANT SHALL MAKE RESTITUTION IN AMOUNT TO BE DETERMINED BY PROBATION OFFICER.*
10/21/2010	Conversion Event *SEPRF:* *DEFENDANT IS ORDERED TO PAY A $200.00 PROBATION REVOCATION FINE PURSUANT TO SECTION 1202.44 OF THE PENAL CODE. STAYED PENDING SUCCESSFUL COMPLETION OF PROBATION.*
10/21/2010	Conversion Event *PRDDW:* *DEFENDANT SHALL NOT OWN OR POSSESS DANGEROUS OR DEADLY WEAPONS AND OR FIREARMS.*
10/21/2010	Conversion Event *PROTH:* *OR AMMUNITION*
10/21/2010	Conversion Event *PRNOC:* *DEFENDANT SHALL NOT CONTACT, CALL OR OTHERWISE COMMUNICATE WITH VICTIM DURING PROBATION PERIOD.*
10/21/2010	Conversion Event *PRATC:* *DEFENDANT ACCEPTED TERMS AND CONDITIONS OF PROBATION.*
10/21/2010	Conversion Event *MI296:* *GENETIC MARKER TESTING PURSUANT TO PC 296 IS ORDERED.*
10/21/2010	Conversion Event *SEASE:* *ALL ORIGINAL SENTENCE ELEMENTS FOR THIS PROCEEDINGS ENTERED.*
10/21/2010	Conversion Event *MICMS:* *ENTERED ON CJIS BY KWOMACK DATE 10 22 2010 .*
10/21/2010	Protective order pursuant to Section 136.2 ordered and filed *FDPRO:* *PROTECTIVE ORDER IN CRIMINAL PROCEEDINGS PURSUANT TO SEC. 136.2 OF THE PENAL CODE ORDERED AND FILED.*

10/21/2010	Conversion Event *MIPPA:* *PERSON TO BE RESTRAINED CARLOS ARTURO CAMPOS*
10/21/2010	Conversion Event *MIPPD:* *THIS PROCEEDING WAS HEARD ON 10 15 2010 AT 1:30 P.M. IN DEPT: 33 BY JUDICIAL OFFICER GARRATT*
10/21/2010	Conversion Event *MIPPU:* *THE ORDER EXPIRES ON 10 15 2013*
10/21/2010	Conversion Event *MIORM:* *DEFENDANT WAS PERSONALLY SERVED WITH A COPY OF THE PROTECTIVE ORDER AT THE COURT HEARING AND NO ADDITIONAL PROOF OF SERVICE OF THIS ORDER IS REQUIRED.*
10/21/2010	Conversion Event *MIORJ:* *COMPLETE NAMES OF THE PROTECTED PERSONS: EDGAR PENALOZA*
10/21/2010	Conversion Event *MIORN:* *GOOD CAUSE APPEARING, THE COURT ORDERS THAT THE ABOVE- NAMED DEFENDANT MUST NOT HARASS, STRIKE, THREATEN, ASSAULT (SEXUALLY OR OTHERWISE), FOLLOW, STALK, MOLEST, DESTROY OR DAMAGE PERSONAL OR REAL PROPERTY, DISTURB THE PEACE, KEEP UNDER SURVEILLANCE, OR BLOCK MOVEMENTS OF THE PROTECTED PERSONS NAMED ABOVE.*
10/21/2010	Conversion Event *MIORO:* *GOOD CAUSE APPEARING, THE COURT ORDERS THAT THE ABOVE- NAMED DEFENDANT MUST SURRENDER TO LOCAL LAW ENFORCEMENT OR SELL TO A LICENSED GUN DEALER ANY FIREARM OWNED OR SUBJECT TO HIS OR HER IMMEDIATE POSSESSION OR CONTROL WITHIN 24 HOURS AFTER SERVICE OF THIS ORDER AND MUST FILE A RECEIPT WITH THE COURT SHOWING COMPLIANCE WITH THIS ORDER WITHIN 48 HOURS OF RECEIVING THIS ORDER.*
10/21/2010	Conversion Event *MIORD:* *GOOD CAUSE APPEARING, THE COURT ORDERS THE ABOVE-NAMED DEFENDANT MUST NOT ATTEMPT TO OR ACTUALLY PREVENT OR DISSUADE ANY VICTIM OR WITNESS FROM ATTENDING A HEARING OR TESTIFYING OR MAKING A REPORT TO ANY LAW ENFORCEMENT AGENCY OR PERSON.*
10/21/2010	Conversion Event *MIORP:* *GOOD CAUSE APPEARING, THE COURT ORDERS THAT THE ABOVE- NAMED DEFENDANT MUST TAKE NO ACTION TO OBTAIN THE ADDRESSES OR LOCATIONS OR PROTECTED PERSONS OR THEIR FAMILY MEMBERS, CARETAKERS, OR GUARDIAN UNLESS GOOD CAUSE EXISTS OTHERWISE.*
10/21/2010	Conversion Event *MIORE:* *GOOD CAUSE APPEARING, THE COURT ORDERS THE ABOVE-NAMED DEFENDANT MUST HAVE NO PERSONAL, TELEPHONIC, OR WRITTEN CONTACT WITH THE PROTECTED PERSONS NAMED ABOVE.*
10/21/2010	Conversion Event *MIORF:*

	GOOD CAUSE APPEARING. THE COURT ORDERS THE ABOVE-NAMED DEFENDANT MUST HAVE NO CONTACT WITH THE PROTECTED PERSONS NAMED BELOW THROUGH A THIRD PARTY, EXCEPT AN ATTORNEY OF RECORD.
10/21/2010	Conversion Event *MIORG:* *GOOD CAUSE APPEARING. THE COURT ORDERS THE ABOVE-NAMED DEFENDANT, MUST NOT COME WITHIN 100 YARDS OF THE PROTECTED PERSONS NAMED ABOVE.*
10/21/2010	Conversion Event *MIORV:* *THE PROTECTED PERSONS MAY RECORD ANY PROHIBITED COMMUNICATIONS MADE BY THE RESTRAINED PERSON.*
10/21/2010	Conversion Event *SEASE:* *ALL ORIGINAL SENTENCE ELEMENTS FOR THIS PROCEEDINGS ENTERED.*
10/21/2010	Conversion Event *MICMS:* *ENTERED ON CJIS BY KWOMACK DATE 10 22 2010.*
10/21/2010	**Disposition** 001. PC245(A)(1)-FEL-ASSAULT W/DEADLY WEAPON OTHER THAN FIREARM OR GBI FORCE Certified to Superior Court: PN859 Charge #: 001 Allegation:
10/21/2010	**Plea** (Judicial Officer: SUPERIOR COURT JUDGE, SAN MATEO COUNTY) 001. PC245(A)(1)-FEL-ASSAULT W/DEADLY WEAPON OTHER THAN FIREARM OR GBI FORCE No Contest / Nolo Contendere Charge #: 001 Allegation:
11/01/2010	Conversion Event *APDAD:* *DEPUTY DA MORLEY B. PITT DESIGNATED AS PROSECUTING ATTORNEY OF RECORD.*
11/30/2010	Conversion Event *SHRST:* *VACATE, THAT WAS SET ON 12 02 2010 AT 8:45 A.M. AND RESET TO 12 02 2010 AT 8:45 A.M. IN SCRWC, D- CR FOR RESTITUTION REPORT.*
11/30/2010	Conversion Event *SHVHG:* *VACATE RESTITUTION REPORT SET IN SUPERIOR COURT ON 12 02 2010 AT 8:45 A.M.*
12/06/2010	Conversion Event *SHHRG:* *MATTER IS SET ON 12 15 2010 AT 8:45 A.M. IN SCRWC COURT. D- CR FOR RESTITUTION REPORT.*
12/06/2010	Conversion Event *MISCE:* *SET AT REQUEST OF ATTY BUENAVENTURA*
12/06/2010	Conversion Event *MICMS:* *ENTERED ON CJIS BY EESPINOZA DATE 12 06 2010*

12/15/2010 | Conversion Event
HHELD:
HEARING HELD ON 12 15 10 AT 8:45 A.M. IN SUPERIOR COURT - HALL OF JUSTICE & RECORDS . D-13 , HON. LISA A NOVAK JUDGE , PRESIDING. CLERK: FRANCOISE ESPINOZA . REPORTER: STACY GASKILL . CLERK2: ANDREA DALEY . DEPUTY D.A. MCKOWAN . DEFENSE COUNSEL PRESENT: BUENAVENTURA .

12/15/2010 | Conversion Event
HHRER:
RESTITUTION REPORT

12/15/2010 | Conversion Event
APDFB:
DEFENDANT PRESENT IN CUSTODY.

12/15/2010 | Conversion Event
APINT:
DIAZ PRESENT AND DULY SWORN HAS OATH ON FILE AS SPANISH LANGUAGE INTERPRETER.

12/15/2010 | Conversion Event
APPDA:
PRIVATE DEFENDER APPOINTED ATTORNEY OF RECORD, WITH BUENAVENTURA DESIGNATED.

12/15/2010 | Conversion Event
PRMOD.
PROBATION MODIFIED AS FOLLOWS:

12/15/2010 | Conversion Event
PROTH:
PAY RESTITUTION TO EDGAR PENALOZA, IN THE AMOUNT OF $2,494.76, PLUS A 10% ADMINISTRATIVE FEE, PAYABLE JOINTLY AND SEVERALLY WITH CO-DEFENDANT JOSE LUIS RODRIGUEZ. PAYABLE THRU PROABTION AS DIRECTED.

12/15/2010 | Conversion Event
PRRIE:
ALL OTHER PREVIOUSLY ORDERED TERMS AND CONDITIONS OF PROBATION TO REMAIN IN EFFECT.

12/15/2010 | Conversion Event
PRATC:
DEFENDANT ACCEPTED TERMS AND CONDITIONS OF PROBATION.

12/15/2010 | Conversion Event
SEDSS:
DEFENDANT IS SERVING SENTENCE.

12/15/2010 | Conversion Event
SEAME:
ALL SENTENCE MODIFICATIONS FOR THIS PROCEEDING ENTERED.

12/15/2010 | Conversion Event
MICMS:
ENTERED ON CJIS BY A DALEY DATE 12 15 2010 .

12/20/2010 | Conversion Event
MISCE:
INTER-DEPARTMENTAL CORRESPONDENCE RESTITUTION REPORT

12/23/2010 | Conversion Event

	FDTCP: *CONDITIONS OF PROBATION FILED*
02/17/2011	Conversion Event *FDAPW:* *AFFIDAVIT OF PROBATION VIOLATION AND MOTION FOR ISSUANCE OF BENCH WARRANT FILED.*
02/17/2011	Conversion Event *BWRSN:* *VOP ON 02 17 2011 FOR SUPERVISED PROBATION ORDER*
02/17/2011	Conversion Event *FDRPR:* *RECOMMENDATION FROM PROBATION DEPARTMENT RECEIVED.*
02/17/2011	Conversion Event *PWPSD:* *ORDER REVOKING PROBATION, DIRECTING ISSUANCE OF BENCH WARRANT AND BENCH WARRANT ISSUED. NO BAIL. WARRANT SIGNED BY NOVAK, LISA A.,*
02/18/2011	Conversion Event *BATCH:* *AWS SVC. ACTION ON 02 18 2011 AT 19:02 BY 41100. J16112 NEW WARRANT STATUS IS: OUTSTANDING -- ACTIVE STATUS UPDATED IN CJIS ON: 02 21 2011*
06/09/2011	Conversion Event *FDMIS:* *ORDER RECALLING BENCH WARRANT FILED.*
06/09/2011	Conversion Event *PRREA:* *PROBATION IS REINSTATED FOR THE SAME PERIOD AND ON THE SAME TERMS AND CONDITIONS.*
06/10/2011	Conversion Event *WWORW:* *BENCH WARRANT ISSUED ON 02 17 2011 , RECALLED ON 06 10 2011 .*
06/10/2011	Conversion Event *BATCH:* *AWS SVC. ACTION ON 06 10 2011 AT 15:43 BY 0413J. J16112 NEW WARRANT STATUS IS: RECALLED STATUS UPDATED IN CJIS ON: 06 13 2011*
06/22/2011	Conversion Event *WWRAB:* *ARREST WARRANT BENCH WARRANT ISSUED ON 02 17 2011 , RETURNED AND FILED.*
03/08/2014	Conversion Event *MICH:* *CH FORWARDED TO ARRESTING AGENCY AND DEPARTMENT OF JUSTICE.*

Exhibit '7'

Removal Order of the Applicant from July 2011

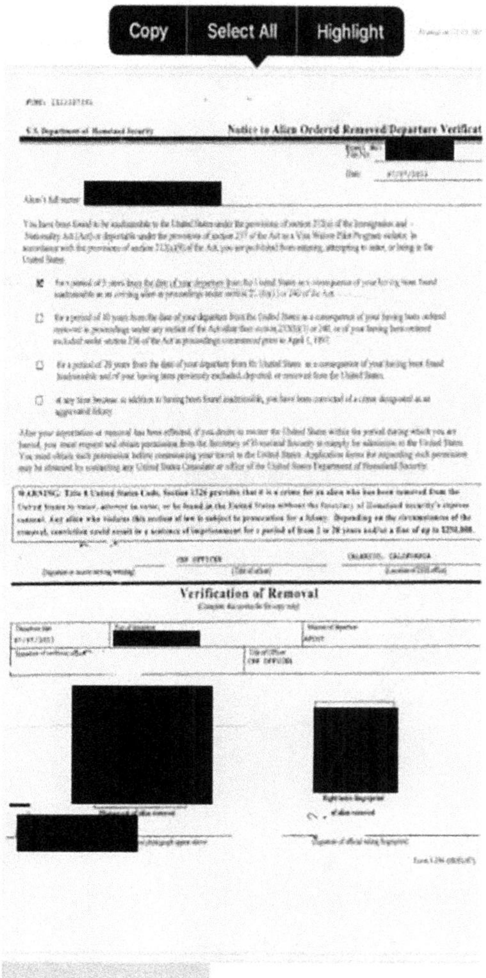

Copy | Select All | Highlight

U.S. Department of Homeland Security

Notice to Alien Ordered Removed/Departure Verificat

Alien's full name:

WARNING: Title 8 United States Code, Section 1326 provides that it is a crime for an alien who has been removed from the United States to enter, attempt to enter, or be found in the United States without the Secretary of Homeland Security's express consent. Any alien who violates this section of law is subject to prosecution for a felony. Depending on the circumstances of the removal, conviction could result in a sentence of imprisonment for a period of from 2 to 20 years and/or a fine of up to $250,000.

CBP OFFICER

Verification of Removal

CBP OFFICER

Form I-296

Exhibit '8'

Letter of Support from Friends and Family of the Applicant

June 6th, 2018

To whom it may concern,

My name is Florence Dispensa and I'm writing this letter to inform you about my good friend [redacted]. I have known [redacted] for 12 years. He is a good man, great father to 3 beautiful kids, & great husband to my best friend. He always takes care and supports his family lovingly and financially. [redacted] is unbelievably talented and very smart. He is a very hard dedicated worker. He has so many skills. He can fix a variety of things. You name it, he could do it. When someone needs help he is just a call away. [redacted] is also the godfather of my daughter and he also helps watch my son every now and then when needed. [redacted] is a great friend and is family to me. He is very adventurous and loves being outdoors and traveling. Every now and then our families make plans to go camping and or do fireworks on 4th of July, go to Las Vegas. [redacted] is someone I can always rely on and always trust.

Thank you for taking the time to read my letter.

Best regards,

Florence Dispensa

6/6/2018

Luis Rodriguez

To whom it may concern

My name is Luis Rodriguez, I am a U.S. citizen I currently live in . . I have known for a really long time, since and my brother used to go to high school. has always been an incredible person and more than a friend, he is part of our family. I've shared great memories with from different stages of our lives, from our early days to building our families and paassing our friendship along to our kids. I have the honor to be the godfather of one of his kids.

is a hard working individual, a great humble person and an excellent father and husband with a great moral character. He is family oriented and a great asset to our community. is the type of person who's fully involved with his community and along his peers.

sets a very good sample in our society. If you have any questions in regards to please do not hesitate to contact me.

I declare under penalty of perjury under the laws of the United States that the foregoing, is true and correct to the best of my knowledge.

Respectfully,

Luis Rodriguez

6/6/2018

Janet Gomez

To whom it may concern

My name is Janet Gomez , I am a U.S. citizen I currently live in . . I met through my husband, they have been friends for a really long time, more than friends they are like family. has a great family that supports him throughly and depend of him. has two sons and a daughter who motivate him in every aspect of his ife. Our families have shared great moments together and look forward for more to come in the future.

has always been a positive asset and a great role model. He works hard to provide for his family. he is a caring human being and a great father.

sets a very good sample in our society. If you have any questions in regards to please do not hesitate to contact me.

I declare under penalty of perjury under the laws of the United States that the foregoing, is true and correct to the best of my knowledge.

Respectfully,

Janet Gomez

(

To whom it may concern,

My name is ████ ████ I've been knowing ████ ████ for a long time now. Not only is he a great person, but he's a great friend and father as well. He does a lot to help anybody that needs help. He's always there if you need a favor. I used to work with ████ at a bread factory and I remember how great he made the atmosphere feel. Never got into any arguments with anyone. Such a hardworking man. Always providing for his family in Mexico and wife and kids as well. I'm so lucky to have a great person like him in my life

Sincerely,

Esther ████

June 25 2018

My name is Ricardo Medina I been knowing him since 2008. I had an accident on that year after waking up from coma since I remember meeting him he been a great friend helping me on my recovery and taking me to my appointments I will always be thankful. We became really good friends we have a bond like brothers. He loves his kids and wife there are his world. I know if I need him hell be there to help me with anything I need. He is caring and very intelligent guy.

Ricardo medina

June 25,2018

My name is Karina ████ and I know ████ ████ all my life. He is my cousin he is a great person and friend. He is the god father of my baby girl Khloe medina. The reason I choose him to be is because I know that he will take care of her if one day I am not here. He is a loving and caring and those qualities I love.

He love his kids and wife more than anything in this world and does anything to make them happy.

After the accident happened we noticed big change in ████ he doesn't want to come to my house in Oakland California anymore he is afraid for his life and he looks more sad.

I was a witnesses of the day of the accident they came to my house to visit but they ended up being assaulted the wife, the daughter and my cousin ████

Karina ████

June 1, 2018

Yo conosi a [redacted] [redacted] mi llerno cuando mi hija [redacted] a mi casa ase 10 anos ami me gusto como trataba ami hija siempre le compraba un oso siempre la cuidaba mucho asta el dia de hoy siempre ah sido asi el. y ahora con su familia la proteje y cuida mucho, es muy trabajador muy Buena gente el es muy listo y sabe de muchas cosas.

Mi esposo y yo lo queremos mucho Como si fuera nuestro hijo y le damos gracias ah dios por poner un Hombre asi para mi hija.

Virginia [redacted]

June 15, 2018

To whom it may concern,

My name is [redacted] I was born in fair field California I am 24 years old. I am typing this letter to talk about my husband [redacted] I meant my husband back in September of 2009 and now we have 3 kids together my oldest son name is [redacted] my second is [redacted] and my third is my precious baby girl [redacted] they have a beautiful and bright names because they are bright and with a lot of life ahead of them. I and my husband are really strict when it comes to education but we are really relaxed parents that love to play like kids with them because we are young also.

My husband is a hardworking individual that dreams and has a lot of plans even though he don't have a green card my husband has goals and I know he will accomplishes them because he that type of guy that don't give up . "With god everything is possible" [redacted] is a person that likes to help without getting nothing back. My husband is a member of the PTA meeting for my sons school Belle Air. My husband fixes random things, he is very smart you would be surprised how smart he is when it comes to fixing things like (plumbing, mechanic, electricity, auto body, construction, landscaping and so many other things. He is such a fast learner he is a great person for our community.

We are a catholic family that are close to god and that have faith. My husband is family man that's has always demonstrated that his family is always first and that he loves his kids with all his heart.

He loves playing video games and basketball he likes to take my son to catholic school every Saturday for my oldest son preparation to do his first communion.

On January 27 2018 our life's changed completely my husband, my 1 year old daughter and I were involved in a robbery assault. I've never felt so much fear in my life. We were all in danger "we could've been killed" I would've never made it back to my boys "thank god we are here". But since that day my husband and myself walk with fear, we can't sleep and if we sleep with have nightmares of that day. We also don't go out anymore and I been getting depression really bad were I can't stop crying.

My biggest fear now is to lose my husband I don't know what I will do without him he supports me in everything. I don't not have my parents near me anymore, my sister is still a minor and yes I might have friends but I can't depend on them ,nothing in this life is free and me buy myself here would be very hard for me to support my kids my husband is my best friend my lover my everything . My kids would be crushed if they didn't see his father everyday anymore. The only way we could stay together is moving to Mexico. Which I would probably have to if he gets deported.

Living in Mexico were there not much jobs is very hard to support a family of 5.

I know because when my husband got deported back in January 2, 2011 I had to move to Mexico with my oldest son ████ to be with his daddy he was only 10 months. It was the hardest time of my life especially because I am not use to a different country it's a different environment when I first got there I acknowledge the streets and the neighborhood scary looking and dirty. When I first got to my husband grandma house were we wear living I wanted to take a shower and there was no water heater because in Mexico there expensive. So I needed to take a cold shower. For my baby I would warm water up in the stove. But what really got to me was that I didn't have money to buy Enfamil baby formula one of the best formula that are close to breast milk. In Mexico it's really expensive and I had to change my son milk to something cheaper but even though I still didn't have money to buy it. I needed to sell my clothing to make money for my son diapers and formula. It was really sad how my son had a lot of nice expensive Jordan's and at the end they were all ripped with holes and I couldn't buy him anymore.

In Mexico we won't be able to give the life my 3 U.S.A Citizens kids deserve the education my kids deserve my kids have dreams to be a police officers, doctors and in Mexico it will be very hard they will be in a risk of cartels. The government of Mexico doesn't have much rules and the police officers are so corrupt. For example "baby's that are 3 months without car seats "driving you see it everywhere it very dangerous in general.

It's been 9 years since he went to jail and got deported my husband has made mistakes in his young life we didn't know much of laws we didn't know how to fight back my husband case because we were young. But everyone can make mistakes no one is perfect. The most important is to learn from your mistakes. My husband really did learn his lesson and he changed his life completely for his family and became closer to god.

I think everyone deserves a second chance.

GOD BLESS YOU SINCERELY,

████████

████████
████

June 11, 2018

To whom this may concern,

Well I am very pleased to be writing this reference letter on behalf of my family member [redacted] [redacted]

My name is Daniela [redacted] and it is a privilege for me that I have known [redacted] for all my life since he is my cousin. I consider him as a great person, and a hardworking man. [redacted] is a very generous and kind. Along with that he is a family man, He is married and has three children whom he loves and strives for better each and everyday for his family. He is very crafty and knows how to fix thing when are broken. He loves working on cars he is always busy I can always count on him when i need something or help on my broken items.

[redacted] is a very important person in our lives. He always has a smile on his face whenever anyone asks for a favor he never says no. He has also helped his parents and family in mexico for a long time with for example, money, food, and paying bills. He is a responsible loving, Cousin, father, husband and Son. I am so grateful to have him as a family member in my life.

To conclude, thats why its a great honor for me to consider him as a great family member of mines.

Sincerely

____

Daniela [redacted]

June 6, 2018

To whom it may concern,

I Guillermo Quant live in 528 3rd Ave san Bruno California I met my neighbor [redacted] A[redacted] when They moved about 9 years ago. [redacted] [redacted] is a very responsible person and hardworking individually He looks after his family but also his neighborhood he has helped me with my cars mechanic problems, My garden, my electricity problems ext. without charging me because he a friendly human bean. We been involved with family gatherings and it's always been a Pleasure of spending time with is Respectful family.

Best regards, Guillermo Quant

05/26/18

To whom it may concern,

My name is Diego Chamorro I live in 553 3rd Ave San Bruno I been knowing my neighbor for about 8 Years now, we started to get to know each other when I saw him tinting his windows in his garage and I Asked him if he could do it for me and his answer was yes right way.

He's an awesome neighbor that helps without him getting anything back he's a smart guy that knows a Lot about auto body. He also offered to check his house camera's for my dad to see if someone at night Went inside my dad car.

He a friendly guy and great for the community and I can tell he loves his family to death.

Exhibit '9'

Photographs of the Applicant and his Family

Exhibit '10'

World Report 2017: Mexico – Human Rights Watch

LANGUAGE

Mexico

Events of 2017

Mexican marine soldiers guard an area after a shootout between gang members and the Mexican army in Mexico City, Mexico Ju 2017.

AVAILABLE IN

During the administration of President Enrique Peña Nieto, which began in 2012, security forces have been implicated in repeated, serious human rights violations during efforts to combat organized crime—including extrajudicial killings, enforced disappearances, and torture. The government has made little progress in prosecuting those responsible for recent abuses, let alone the large number of abuses committed by soldiers and police since former President Felipe Calderón initiated Mexico's "war on drugs" in 2006.

In April, the Mexican Congress passed legislation to curb torture and the use of coerced evidence during judicial proceedings. Implementation of the law

Enforced Disappearances

Since 2006, Mexico's security forces have carried out widespread enforced disappearances.

In August 2017, the government reported that the whereabouts of more than 32,000 people who had gone missing since 2006 remain unknown. Prosecutors and police routinely fail to take basic investigative steps to identify those responsible for enforced disappearances, often telling the missing people's families to investigate on their own. Authorities have routinely failed to identify remains of bodies or body parts found in various locations, including in clandestine graves, throughout the country.

The federal government has pursued potentially promising initiatives to find people who have gone missing, but they have produced limited results. In 2013, it created a unit in the Attorney General's Office to investigate disappearances, which became a Special Prosecutor's Office in October 2015. However, the office has made only limited progress in investigating and prosecuting cases of forced disappearance.

In 2015, Congress approved a constitutional reform giving it authority to pass general laws on enforced disappearances and torture that would establish a single nationwide definition for each of the crimes and facilitate their prosecution in all 31 states and Mexico City. The law was passed in November 2017. At time of writing, its implementation remained pending.

Mexican authorities have failed to make progress in determining what happened to 43 missing students from the teachers college in Ayotzinapa who disappeared in 2014 and are believed killed. Only one of the students has been positively identified among remains that the government says are those of the students. The Attorney General's Office has failed to conduct in-depth investigations following recommendations made by the Interdisciplinary Group of Independent Experts (GIEI), established through an agreement between the government and the Inter-American Commission on Human Rights (IACHR).

At time of writing, more than 100 people had been charged with alleged involvement in the abductions, yet prosecutors had neither presented accusations against state or federal authorities nor against members of the armed forces, despite indications of their involvement.

An August 2016 internal report from the Attorney General's Office about the Ayotzinapa investigations established that investigators had broken the law and had engaged in arbitrary detentions and the coercion of alleged suspects. The inspector general who wrote the report claimed that the Attorney General's Office asked him to step down shortly after he presented the report to his superiors. The report was rewritten, and the version that the Attorney General's Office eventually published concluded that only a handful of minor violations had been committed.

Extrajudicial Killings

Unlawful killings of civilians by Mexican security forces "take place at an alarmingly high rate" amid an atmosphere of "systematic and endemic impunity," according to the United Nations special rapporteur on extrajudicial, summary, or arbitrary executions in 2014.

In August 2016, the National Human Rights Commission (CNDH) concluded that federal police arbitrarily executed 22 of 42 civilians who died in a confrontation in 2015 in Tanhuato, Michoacán State. Police fatally shot at least 13 people in the back, tortured two detainees, and burned a man alive, the CNDH concluded, then altered the crime scene by moving bodies and planting guns to justify the illegal killings. At time of writing, nobody had been charged and a federal investigation into the Tanhuato killings remained

Military Abuses and Impunity

Mexico has relied heavily on the military to fight drug-related violence and organized crime, leading to widespread human rights violations by military personnel. As of July 2016, the CNDH had received almost 10,000 complaints of abuse by the army since 2006—including more than 2,000 during the current administration. It found in more than 100 cases that military personnel committed serious human rights violations.

In November 2017, the Chamber of Deputies approved the Law on Internal Security, authorizing military involvement in domestic law enforcement activities—including intelligence gathering—without including meaningful measures to improve accountability. At time of writing, the proposal was under discussion in the Senate.

In 2014, Congress reformed the Code of Military Justice to require that abuses committed by members of the military against civilians be handled by the civilian criminal justice system rather than the military system, which had a history of routinely failing to hold members of the military accountable for abuses.

In May 2016, provisions included in a new Military Code of Criminal Procedure and in reforms to the Code of Military Justice granted military prosecutors and judges broad powers to order the search of homes and public buildings, and to listen to private telecommunications, without a judicial order issued by a civilian judge. In June 2016, the CNDH challenged the constitutionality of these provisions. At time of writing, a Supreme Court decision was still pending.

In the case of Tlatlaya, where soldiers killed 22 civilians in 2014—witnesses and the CNDH reported that they extrajudicially executed at least 12 of them —nobody has been convicted of the killings. In May 2016, a civilian, federal court absolved the last of eight soldiers charged with homicide. However, in July 2017, a judge ordered the Attorney General's Office to investigate the case in-depth, including the responsibility of military commanders and the

Torture

Torture is widely practiced in Mexico to obtain confessions and extract information. It is most frequently applied in the period between when victims are detained, often arbitrarily, and when they are handed over to civilian prosecutors, a period in which they are often held incommunicado at military bases or illegal detention sites.

According to a survey of more than 64,000 people incarcerated in 370 Mexican prisons located throughout the country in 2016, performed by Mexico's national statistics office (Instituto Nacional de Estadística y Geografía – INEGI), 57.8 percent of the prison population reported having suffered some type of physical violence at the time of their arrest. Of these people, 19 percent reported receiving electrical shocks; 36 percent being choked, held underwater, or smothered; and 59 percent being hit or kicked. In addition, 28 percent reported that they were threatened that their family would be harmed.

In April 2017, the Mexican legislature approved the Law to Investigate, Prevent, and Sanction Torture, aimed at curbing torture and excluding testimony obtained through torture from judicial proceedings. At time of writing, implementation of the law remained pending.

As of June 30, 2017, the Specialized Unit for the Investigation of the Crime of Torture—a unit within the Attorney General's Office—had 4,390 ongoing investigations into alleged cases of torture. Additionally, between September 2016 and June 2017, courts ordered more than 750 criminal investigations into allegations of torture.

The Interdisciplinary Group of Independent Experts, established through an agreement between the government and the IACHR concluded in April 2016 that 80 percent of the suspects detained in connection with the Ayotzinapa case showed bodily injuries possibly due to ill treatment and torture. As of September 2017, the Attorney General's Office was conducting six investigations related to the alleged torture of 31 people. None of the

According to the CNDH, Mexico State prosecutors sought to cover up military wrongdoing in the Tlatlaya case by using torture to coerce false testimony from witnesses. Four police officers were sentenced to three years and eight months' imprisonment for the crime. As of September 2017—more than three years after the massacre—nobody has been convicted in connection with the cover-up.

Criminal Justice System

The criminal justice system routinely fails to provide justice to victims of violent crimes and human rights violations. Causes of failure include corruption, inadequate training and resources, and complicity of prosecutors and public defenders with criminals and abusive officials. The failure of law enforcement has contributed to the emergence of armed citizen self-defense groups in several parts of the country.

In 2013, Mexico enacted a federal Victims Law intended to ensure justice, protection, and reparations for crime victims. Reforms to the law, intended to reduce bureaucracy and improve access to aid and reparations for victims, were approved in January 2017.

Attacks on Journalists and Human Rights Defenders

Journalists, particularly those who report on crime or criticize officials, face harassment and attack by both government authorities and criminal groups. Journalists are often driven to self-censorship as a result.

From 2000 through October 2017, 104 journalists were killed and 25 disappeared, according to the Attorney General's Office. The nongovernmental organization (NGO) Article 19 documented eight cases of journalists killed and one disappeared between January and July 2017.

Authorities routinely fail to investigate crimes against journalists adequately, often preemptively ruling out their profession as a motive. The CNDH reported in 2016 that 90 percent of crimes against journalists in Mexico since 2000 have gone unpunished, including 82 percent of killings and 100 percent of disappearances. Since its creation in July 2010, the Special Prosecutor's Office for Crimes against Freedom of Expression has opened more than 1,000 investigations into crimes against journalists. As of October 2017, it has brought charges in 115 cases and obtained only 3 convictions.

In July 2017, an investigation by Citizen Lab, a research center at the University of Toronto, showed that at least 11 human rights activists and journalists (as well as the 16-year-old son of a journalist) and members of the GIEI had been targets of a spyware campaign conducted with sophisticated software bought by the Mexican government. A senator and two high-ranking members of the main opposition party were also targeted. The affected activists filed complaints with the Attorney General's Office, which opened an investigation.

By October 2016, 617 people had received protection under a 2012 law to protect journalists and human rights defenders. However, protection has been slow to arrive or, in some cases, insufficient.

Women's and Girls' Rights

Mexican laws do not adequately protect women and girls against domestic and sexual violence. Some provisions, including those that make the severity of punishments for some sexual offenses contingent upon the "chastity" of the victim, contradict international standards.

Eighteen of Mexico's 31 states have passed laws establishing that there is a right to life from the moment of conception. Although the Supreme Court ruled in 2010 that all states must provide emergency contraception and access to abortion for rape victims, many women and girls face serious barriers accessing abortions after sexual violence, including official intimidation.

Unaccompanied Migrant Children

Apprehensions of unaccompanied children from the Northern Triangle countries of El Salvador, Guatemala, and Honduras decreased sharply in the first seven months of 2017 compared with the same period in 2016, and asylum recognition rates for unaccompanied children from these countries have risen in recent years. Even so, less than 1 percent of those apprehended each year received international protection, far short of the likely need: the UN High Commissioner for Refugees (UNHCR) has estimated that as many as half of the unaccompanied children who arrive in Mexico from the Northern Triangle have plausible asylum claims that should be seriously considered.

Sexual Orientation and Gender Identity

Same-sex marriage has been legal in Mexico City since 2010. It is also permitted in 10 additional states (eight of which have reformed their local legislation to allow it and two where the Supreme Court invalidated articles of the local Civil Code, therefore permitting it without a legislative change). In 2015, the Supreme Court opened the door to recognition in all states by ruling that defining marriage exclusively as a union between a man and a woman constitutes discrimination and thus violates Mexico's Constitution.

In May 2016, President Peña Nieto introduced bills to recognize same-sex marriage in the constitution and the Federal Civil Code. This would have also removed sexual orientation and gender identity as barriers to adoption. However, the federal bill was rejected when two committees in the Chamber of Deputies voted against the initiative in November 2016.

At the same time, President Peña Nieto instructed federal agencies to recognize gender identity through the reissuance of birth certificates and passports, without a doctor's involvement. He also instructed the Secretariat of Education to include sexual diversity among the new educational materials. It had yet to do so at time of writing.

Disability Rights

In a 2014 report, the UN Committee on the Rights of Persons with Disabilities found that, despite new laws and programs protecting the rights of the disabled, serious gaps remained, including in access to justice, legal standing, and the right to vote; access to buildings, transportation, and

In 2015, Disability Rights International reported that conditions were inhumane in Mexico City's government-funded facilities for people with disabilities, including one institution that locked children in cages. The report also documented that women with psychosocial disabilities at state-run clinics in Mexico City were sometimes pressured into being sterilized or, when pregnant, into having abortions.

Mexico made no progress in the implementation of the right to legal capacity for persons with disabilities. In addition, it amended the General Education Law in June 2016, enabling the special education of children with disabilities in schools.

In February 2016, Mexico's Supreme Court determined the requirement that people on the autistic spectrum obtain a certificate of ability to work violates Mexico's Constitution, as well as international human rights standards.

Key International Actors

In September, the UN Committee on Migrant Workers published a preliminary report in which it expressed its concern about the "grave irregularities" in the identification of the victims and those responsible for the mass murders of migrants committed between 2010 and 2012 in the states of Nuevo León and Tamaulipas. It also urged the state to guarantee the rights of migrants in transit and called upon Mexican authorities to "only use the detention of migrants as a measure of last resort," to improve conditions of detention, and to "immediately put an end to" the detention of migrant children.

In January, after his visit to the country, the UN special rapporteur on human rights defenders raised concerns about attacks against human rights defenders and criminalization of their activities. In May, the special rapporteurs on freedom of expression from the UN and the IACHR issued a joint statement urging the Mexican government "to end [the] epidemic of violence against journalists."

In April, the UN working group on human rights and business had also urged the government to better protect human rights defenders and journalists, as well as to implement mechanisms to create social dialogue about large-scale projects and improve efforts to combat gender-based discrimination in the workplace.

The IACHR published a report in March 2016 documenting a wide range of abuses in Mexico—including disappearances; extrajudicial executions; torture; and insecurity for women, children, migrants, human rights defenders, and journalists—which they concluded amounted to a "crisis of gross human rights violations." The government criticized the report, responding that there was no "human rights crisis" in Mexico. Later that month, Mexican authorities denied UN Special Rapporteur on Torture Juan Méndez permission to return before the end of his term, rejecting his conclusion that torture was widespread and accusing him of acting "unethically."

In October 2016, the Office of the UN High Commissioner for Human Rights (OHCHR) issued 14 recommendations to Mexico on the need to address impunity for human rights violations, adopt laws to regulate the use of force and eliminate torture and enforced disappearances, and establish an independent forensic institution with adequate resources. In May 2016, the UN special rapporteur on extrajudicial, summary, or arbitrary executions released a report on Mexico identifying continuing serious violations, including extrajudicial killings and excessive use of force by security forces, impunity, and lack of reparations for victims.

Since 2007, the United States has allocated more than US$1.6 billion in aid through the Mérida Initiative to help combat organized crime. In 2015, the

Exhibit '11'

Amnesty International – Mexico Annual Report 2017/2018

AMNESTY INTERNATIONAL

MEXICO 2017/2018

ANNUAL REPORT MEXICO

← Back to Mexico

MEXICO 2017/2018

Violence increased throughout Mexico. The armed forces continued to undertake regular policing functions. Human rights defenders and journalists were threatened, attacked and killed; digital attacks and surveillance were particularly common. Widespread arbitrary detentions continued to lead to torture and other ill-treatment, enforced disappearances and extrajudicial executions. Impunity persisted for human rights violations and crimes under international law. Mexico received a record number of asylum claims, mostly from nationals of El Salvador, Honduras, Guatemala and Venezuela. Violence against women remained a major concern; new data showed that two thirds of women had experienced gender-based violence during their lives. The rights to housing and education were compromised by two major earthquakes.

Background

Early in the year an increase in gas prices caused social unrest, including road blockages, lootings and protests throughout the country, leading to hundreds of arrests and some fatalities. Throughout the year, security forces carried out a number of operations to crack down on a spate of clandestine robberies of petroleum. At least one of these security operations resulted in a likely extrajudicial execution by the army in May. The National Human Rights Commission raised concerns over deficient security measures in prisons that affected the rights of people deprived of their liberty. There were riots in prisons including in the states of

The new adversarial criminal justice system, fully operational since June 2016, continued to replicate problems from the old inquisitorial system, including violations of the presumption of innocence and the use of evidence collected in violation of human rights and other illicit evidence. Bills were introduced in Congress that would weaken fair trial guarantees and expand the scope of mandatory pre-trial detention without a case-by-case assessment by a judge.

Congress approved long-overdue laws against torture and other ill-treatment and against enforced disappearance by state actors and disappearances committed by non-state actors. Legal reforms allowed the use of cannabis for medical purposes. Sustained public debates over the transformation of the federal Attorney General's Office, responsible for law enforcement and prosecution, into an independent body were conducted during the year. In August, civil society organizations and opinion leaders presented a proposal for the design of this institution.

In October, the acting Attorney General removed the Special Prosecutor for Electoral Crimes, regarded as independent by different political forces, after he publicly reported being subjected to political pressure to disregard a high-profile corruption case.

Police and security forces

There was a marked increase in the number of homicides, with 42,583 recorded nationally, the highest annual number of homicides registered by authorities since the start of the presidential term in December 2012. The real number may be higher, with some crimes not being reported to police, and not all of those reported triggering official action.

In December, Congress passed a Law on Interior Security enabling the prolonged presence of the armed forces in regular policing functions without any effective provisions for transparency, accountability or civilian oversight.

Arbitrary arrests and detentions

Arbitrary arrests and detentions remained widespread, and often led to further human rights violations including torture and other ill-treatment, enforced disappearances and extrajudicial executions. Arbitrary arrests often included the planting of evidence, commonly guns and illicit drugs, by law enforcement officials. Authorities appeared to especially target those who had historically faced discrimination, in particular young men living in poverty.

The police routinely disregarded their obligations during and following an arrest. They usually did not inform the persons of the reasons for the arrest or of their rights, such as the right to legal counsel and to communicate with their families. Unjustified delays in bringing the detainee before the relevant authorities were common and often enabled other human rights violations. Police reports of arrests often contained significant errors, fabricated information and other serious flaws, including inaccuracies in recording date and

The reasons for arbitrary arrests were varied, but included: to extort money from detainees; to detain a particular individual in return for payment from a third party; for politically motivated reasons; and to investigate detainees in connection with another crime by detaining them for a misdemeanour that they usually had not committed.

There was no unified and accessible register of detention, consistent with international human rights law and standards, in which every detention by law enforcement officials is recorded in real time.[1]

Torture and other ill-treatment

In February, the UN Special Rapporteur on torture issued a follow-up report to a previous visit to Mexico in 2014; the report concluded that torture and other ill-treatment remained widespread, including the alarming use of sexual violence as a frequent method of torture.

In June, a new general law on torture came into force, replacing existing state and federal laws with nationwide application. Civil society organizations welcomed it as an advance that better incorporated international standards compared to the previous legislation. The Special Unit on Torture of the Federal Attorney General's Office reported 4,390 cases of torture under revision at the federal level and commenced 777 investigations under the new adversarial justice system. Federal authorities did not announce any new criminal charges against public officials, nor provide any information on arrests made for the crime of torture. In Quintana Roo state, a federal judge sentenced a former policeman to five years' imprisonment for the crime of torture.

Enforced disappearances

Enforced disappearances with the involvement of the state and disappearances committed by non-state actors continued to be common and those responsible enjoyed almost absolute impunity. The official National Register of Missing and Disappeared Persons indicated that the fate or whereabouts of 34,656 people (25,682 men and 8,974 women) remained unclarified. The actual numbers were higher because the official figure excluded federal pre-2014 cases and cases classified as other criminal offences such as hostage-taking or human trafficking.

Investigations into cases of missing persons continued to be flawed and authorities generally failed to immediately initiate searches for the victims. Impunity for these crimes continued, including in the case of 43 students from the Ayotzinapa teacher training college who were forcibly disappeared in Guerrero state in 2014. The investigations into the case made little progress during the year. In March, in a hearing before the Inter-American Commission on Human Rights, state representatives reasserted the government's version of events that the students had been killed and burned in a local rubbish dump – a theory that was proved to be scientifically impossible by the Interdisciplinary Group of Independent Experts appointed by the Commission.

In October, Congress passed a general law on disappearances that defined the crime in accordance with

to require a sufficient budget allocation in the following years.

Extrajudicial executions

Cases of extrajudicial executions were not properly investigated and perpetrators continued to enjoy impunity. For the fourth consecutive year, the authorities failed to publish the number of people killed or wounded in clashes with the police and military forces. No information was made available regarding criminal charges in the cases of Tlatlaya, Mexico state, where soldiers killed 22 people in 2014; Apatzingán, Michoacán state, where federal police and other security forces killed at least 16 people in 2015; and Tanhuato, Michoacán state, where the security forces killed 43 people during a security operation in 2015.

On 3 May, military personnel carried out public security operations in Palmarito Tochapan town, Puebla state, and reported that seven people died, including four soldiers. Days later, video footage from security cameras installed at the location were published on the internet. One of the videos clearly showed a person in military uniform shooting dead a man lying on the floor. Amnesty International independently verified the video and concluded that there was sufficient reason to believe that an extrajudicial execution took place.[2]

Refugees' and migrants' rights

A total of 8,703 asylum claims were lodged between January and August, a similar number as for the whole of 2016. The percentage of claims that resulted in the granting of refugee status decreased from 35% in 2016 to 12% in 2017. The majority of asylum claims came from Honduran and Venezuelan nationals, the latter surpassing for the first time the number of refugees and asylum-seekers from El Salvador and Guatemala.

Between January and November, 88,741 irregular migrants were detained and 74,604 deported, in most cases without the opportunity to challenge their deportation. Of those deported, 94% were from Honduras, Guatemala and El Salvador, countries which have registered some of the highest homicide rates in the world in recent years, and 20% of those deported to these countries were children. In February, Mexico's Foreign Minister announced that Mexico would not receive foreign nationals turned back from the USA under the US Border Control Executive Order announced by US President Donald Trump on 25 January.

In June, the government met with North American and Central American governments, ostensibly to tackle the root causes of the regional refugee crisis; they did not publish any agreements reached.

The Unit for the Investigation of Crimes against Migrants of the Attorney General's Office marked two years in operation, yet remained marred by institutional challenges in its operation and problems in co-ordinating with other authorities. These problems limited advances in criminal investigations, including into massacres of migrants, that remained shrouded by impunity.

detention centres run by the Institute. Violations included overcrowding, lack of access to adequate medical services, solitary confinement used as punishment, allegations of torture and other ill-treatment. The authorities denied allegations of torture committed by the Institute, despite the National Human Rights Commission having also confirmed evidence of torture on prior occasions.

Human rights defenders and journalists

Human rights defenders and journalists continued to be threatened, harassed, attacked and killed.

At least 12 journalists were killed, the highest number recorded in one year since 2000. They included prize-winning journalist Javier Valdez, founder of the newspaper *Ríodoce*, who was killed on 15 May in Sinaloa state. Many of the killings of journalists occurred in daylight in public places. The authorities made no significant advances into the investigations of these killings. The Special Prosecutor's Unit for Attention to Crimes against Freedom of Expression failed to investigate the journalists' work as a possible motive in the majority of cases of attacks. The federal Mechanism to Protect Human Rights Defenders and Journalists left human rights defenders and journalists inadequately protected.

Former Goldman Prize winner Isidro Baldenegro López and Juan Ontiveros Ramos, two Indigenous human rights defenders of the Raramuri (Tarahumara) Indigenous People, were killed in January and February respectively. In May, Miriam Rodríguez, a human rights defender leading the search for her daughter and other disappeared persons in Tamaulipas, was killed. In July, Mario Luna Romero, leader of the Indigenous Yaqui People in Sonora state and beneficiary of protection measures from the federal protection mechanism, was subjected to an intrusion in his house by unidentified assailants who set fire to his partner's car.

In January, it became known that a network of people was using the internet to harass and threaten human rights defenders and journalists throughout Mexico.[3] In June, evidence emerged of surveillance against journalists and human rights defenders using software that the government was known to have purchased. The federal Mechanism to Protect Human Rights Defenders and Journalists provided no strategy to respond to digital attacks and unlawful surveillance for those who have been granted protection measures.

Violence against women and girls

Gender-based violence against women and girls was widespread. Most of the cases were inadequately investigated and perpetrators enjoyed impunity. Sufficient and current data on gender-based killings was not available. However, official data for 2016 was published indicating that 2,668 women were considered to be victims of homicide, pending further investigations.

In August, the National Institute of Statistics and Geography published a survey estimating that 66.1% of girls and women aged 15 or above had experienced gender-based violence at least once in their lives, and that 43.5% of women had experienced gender-based violence committed by their partners.

Mechanisms known as "Alerts of gender-based violence against women" were active in 12 states. Established by the General Law on Women's Access to a Life Free from Violence, the Alert mechanisms relied on co-ordinated efforts to confront and eradicate violence against women and girls. By the end of the year, the Alerts mechanisms were not shown to have reduced gender-based violence against women and girls.

Rights of lesbian, gay, bisexual, transgender and intersex people

Same-sex couples were able to marry in Mexico City and 11 states without recourse to judicial proceedings. Couples in states where laws or administrative practice did not allow for same-sex marriage had to file a constitutional complaint (*amparo*) before federal tribunals to have their case reviewed and their rights recognized.

Supreme Court rulings continued to uphold same-sex couples' rights to marry and to adopt children without being discriminated against on the basis of sexual orientation and gender identity. In March, the Supreme Court ruled unconstitutional the Law of the Institute of Security and Social Services for State Workers because it protected only different-sex couples' rights.

Economic, social and cultural rights

Two earthquakes in September had a serious impact on vast areas, mostly in central and southern Mexico. More than 360 people died; in Mexico City the majority of fatalities were women. According to official figures, more than 150,000 households were affected and at least 250,000 people were made homeless.

The government implemented survivor rescue and emergency care actions with the participation of both civil and military personnel and with the support of the international community. However, several reports emerged of inadequate co-ordination among authorities, inaccurate and untimely information on the rescue and recovery of bodies, illegal commandeering of food and other essential services meant for survivors, and insufficient aid deliveries to many devastated areas, especially in small, impoverished communities.

Expert preliminary assessments published in the media suggested that some of the collapsed structures might have been in breach of building regulations. There was no comprehensive strategy to guarantee that people made homeless were provided with safe and adequate housing options. On 6 October, President Peña Nieto called on affected families to organize themselves to rebuild their houses.

Educational services, including many primary schools, were disrupted for weeks or months while safety checks and reconstruction of schools were underway. Thousands of national monuments and other culturally significant public buildings were destroyed or damaged by the earthquakes.

1. False suspicions: Arbitrary detentions by police in Mexico (AMR 41/5340/2017)
2. Mexico: Open letter to the President on a possible extrajudicial execution by the military (AMR

3. Mexico's misinformation wars: How organized troll networks attack and harass journalists and activists in Mexico (News story, 24 January)

GET THE AMNESTY INTERNATIONAL REPORT 2017/18

Choose language

DOWNLOAD PDF

Exhibit '12'

U.S. Department of State – Mexico Travel Advisory 2018

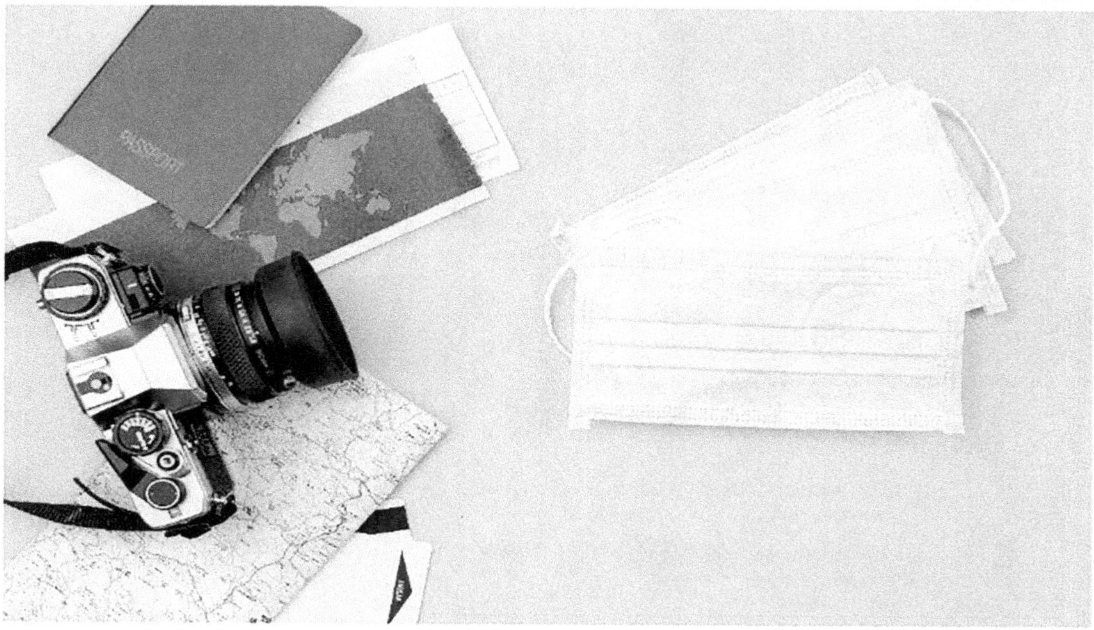

Home | Travel Advisories | Newsroom | About Us | Contact Us | Careers |

Travel.State.Gov

U.S. DEPARTMENT OF STATE — BUREAU OF CONSULAR AFFAIRS

Search

U.S. Passports | International Travel | U.S. Visas | Intercountry Adoption | International Parental Child Abduction

Travel.State.Gov > Travel Advisories > Mexico Travel Advisory

Mexico Travel Advisory

Travel Advisory
March 16, 2018

Mexico - Level 2: Exercise Increased Caution

Exercise increased caution in Mexico due to **crime.** Some areas have increased risk. Read the entire Travel Advisory.

Violent crime, such as homicide, kidnapping, carjacking, and robbery, is widespread.

The U.S. government has limited ability to provide emergency services to U.S. citizens in many areas of Mexico as U.S. government employees are prohibited from travel to these areas.

U.S. government employees are prohibited from intercity travel after dark in many areas of Mexico. U.S. government employees are also not permitted to drive from the U.S.-Mexico border to or from the interior parts of Mexico with the exception of daytime travel on Highway 15 between Nogales and Hermosillo.

Read the Safety and Security section on the country information page.

Do not travel to:

- Colima state due to **crime.**
- Guerrero state due to **crime.**
- Michoacán state due to **crime.**
- Sinaloa state due to **crime.**
- Tamaulipas state due to **crime.**

For all other states in Mexico, please see detailed information below.

If you decide to travel to Mexico:

- Use toll roads when possible and avoid driving at night.
- Exercise increased caution when visiting local bars, nightclubs, and casinos.
- Do not display signs of wealth, such as wearing expensive watches

Travel Advisory Levels

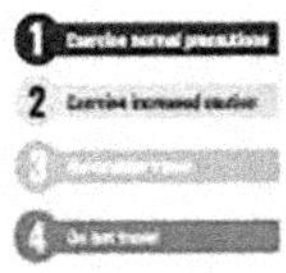

- Enroll in the Smart Traveler Enrollment Program (STEP) to receive Alerts and make it easier to locate you in an emergency.
- Follow the Department of State on Facebook and Twitter.
- Review the Crime and Safety Reports for Mexico.
- U.S. citizens who travel abroad should always have a contingency plan for emergency situations. Review the Traveler's Checklist.

Aguascalientes state – Level 2: Exercise Increased Caution

Exercise increased caution due to crime.

U.S. government employees are prohibited from traveling between cities at night. Additionally, U.S. government employees are prohibited from patronizing adult clubs and gambling establishments in Aguascalientes.

Baja California state – Level 2: Exercise Increased Caution

Exercise increased caution due to crime.

Criminal activity and violence, including homicide, remain an issue throughout the state. According to the Baja California State Secretariat for Public Security, the state experienced an increase in homicide rates compared to the same period in 2016. While most of these homicides appeared to be targeted, criminal organization assassinations, turf battles between criminal groups have resulted in violent crime in areas frequented by U.S. citizens. Bystanders have been injured or killed in shooting incidents.

Due to poor cellular service and hazardous road conditions, U.S. government employees are only permitted to travel on "La Rumorosa" between Mexicali and Tijuana on the toll road during daylight.

There are no U.S. government restrictions in tourist areas in Baja California, which includes: **Ensenada, Rosarito,** and **Tijuana**.

Baja California Sur state – Level 2: Exercise Increased Caution

Exercise increased caution due to crime.

Criminal activity and violence, including homicide, remain an issue throughout the state. According to Government of Mexico statistics, the state experienced an increase in homicide rates compared to the same period in 2016. While most of these homicides appeared to be targeted, criminal organization assassinations, turf battles between criminal groups have resulted in violent crime in areas frequented by U.S. citizens. Bystanders have been injured or killed in shooting incidents.

There are no U.S. government restrictions for travel in Baja California Sur, which includes the tourist areas of **Cabo San Lucas, San Jose del Cabo,** and **La Paz**.

Campeche state – Level 2: Exercise Increased Caution

Exercise increased caution. Police presence and emergency response are extremely limited outside of the state capital.

There are no travel restrictions on U.S. government employees.

Chiapas state – Level 2: Exercise Increased Caution

Exercise increased caution due to crime.

Assistance for U.S. Citizens

U.S. Embassy Mexico City
Paseo de la Reforma 305
Colonia Cuauhtemoc
Mexico, D.F., Mexico C.P. 06500

Telephone
011-52-55-5080-2000

Emergency
American Citizen Services: 01 800 681 9374 (toll free in Mexico) / 81 4160 5512 (from within Mexico) / 844 528 6611 (toll free in the U.S.)

Fax
011-52-55-5080-2201

Email
ACSMexicoCity@state.gov

Website
U.S. Embassy Mexico City

Mexico Map

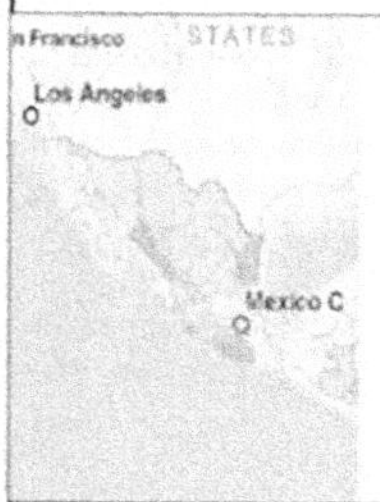

View Larger Map

Search for Travel Advisories

Country or area

There are no restrictions on U.S. government employees in tourist areas in Chiapas state, such as: **Palenque, San Cristobal de las Casas,** and **Tuxtla Gutierrez**.

Chihuahua state – Level 3: Reconsider Travel

Reconsider travel due to crime. Violent crime and gang activity are widespread.

Travel for U.S. government employees is limited to the following areas with the noted restrictions:

- **Ciudad Juarez:** U.S. government employees are prohibited from travel after dark west of Eje Juan Gabriel and south of Boulevard Zaragoza. U.S. government employees are prohibited from travel to the areas southeast of Boulevard Independencia and the Valle de Juarez region.
- **Within the city of Chihuahua:** U.S. government employees are prohibited from travel to the Morelos, Villa, and Zapata districts.
- **Ojinaga:** U.S. government employees must travel via U.S. Highway 67 through the Presidio, Texas port-of-entry.
- **Palomas and the Nuevo Casas Grandes/Paquime region**: U.S. government employees must use U.S. Highway 11 through the Columbus, New Mexico port-of- entry.
- **Nuevo Casas Grandes:** U.S. government employees are prohibited from travel outside city limits after dark.

Visit our website for Travel to High-Risk Areas.

Coahuila state – Level 3: Reconsider Travel

Reconsider travel due to crime. Violent crime is widespread. Local law enforcement has limited capability to prevent and respond to crime, particularly in the northern part of the state.

U.S. government employees are not permitted to travel in Coahuila state, with the exception of Saltillo, Bosques de Monterreal, and Parras de la Fuente. U.S. government employees can only travel to those cities using the most direct routes and maximizing the use of toll highways. Between 1 a.m. and 6 a.m., U.S. government employees must remain within Saltillo, Bosques de Monterreal, or Parras de la Fuente.

U.S. government employees are permitted to travel to Piedras Negras and Ciudad Acuna but they must travel to these cities from the United States only.

U.S. government employees are prohibited from patronizing adult clubs and gambling establishments in Coahuila.

Visit our website for Travel to High-Risk Areas.

Colima state – Level 4: Do Not Travel

Do not travel due to crime. Violent crime and gang activity are widespread.

U.S. government employees are prohibited from travel to Tecoman or within 12 miles of the Colima-Michoacán border and on Route 110 between La Tecomaca and the Jalisco border.

There are no restrictions on U.S. government employees travel along Route

U.S. government employees are prohibited from patronizing adult clubs and gambling establishments in Colima.

Visit our website for Travel to High-Risk Areas.

Durango state – Level 3: Reconsider Travel

Reconsider travel due to crime. Violent crime and gang activity along the highways are common.

U.S. government employees may travel outside the city of Durango only during daylight on toll roads. Between 1 a.m. and 6 a.m., U.S. government employees must remain within Durango city.

U.S. government employees are prohibited from patronizing adult clubs and gambling establishments in Durango.

Visit our website for Travel to High-Risk Areas.

Estado de Mexico state – Level 3: Reconsider Travel

Reconsider travel due to crime. Violent crime is common in parts of Estado de Mexico.

U.S. government employees are prohibited from travel to the following municipalities, unless they are traveling directly through the municipalities on major thoroughfares:

- Coacalco
- Ecatepec
- Nezahualcoyotl
- La Paz
- Valle del Chalco
- Solidaridad
- Chalco
- Ixtapaluca
- Tlatlaya

U.S. government employees are prohibited from travel on any roads between Morelos, Huitzilac, and Santa Martha, Estado de Mexico, including the Lagunas de Zempoala National Park and surrounding areas.

Visit our website for Travel to High-Risk Areas.

Guanajuato state – Level 2: Exercise Increased Caution

Exercise increased caution due to crime.

There are no travel restrictions on U.S. government employees.

Guerrero state – Level 4: Do Not Travel

Do not travel due to crime. Armed groups operate independently of the government in many areas of Guerrero. Members of these groups frequently maintain roadblocks and may use violence towards travelers.

U.S. government employees are prohibited from travel to the entire state of Guerrero, including Acapulco.

Visit our website for Travel to High-Risk Areas.

Exercise increased caution due to crime.

There are no travel restrictions on U.S. government employees.

Jalisco state – Level 3: Reconsider Travel

Reconsider travel due to crime. Violent crime and gang activity are common in parts of Jalisco state.

U.S. government employees are prohibited from travel to areas bordering Michoacán and Zacatecas states. U.S. government employees are prohibited from traveling between cities after dark and from using Highway 80 between Cocula and La Huerta.

U.S. government employees may use federal toll road 15D for travel to Mexico City. However, they may not stop in the towns of La Barca or Ocotlan for any reason.

U.S. government employees are prohibited from patronizing adult clubs and gambling establishments in Jalisco.

There are no restrictions on U.S. government employees for stays in the following tourist areas in Jalisco state: **Guadalajara**, **Puerto Vallarta, Chapala,** and **Ajijic**.

Visit our website for Travel to High-Risk Areas.

Mexico City – Level 2: Exercise Increased Caution

Exercise increased caution due to crime.

There are no travel restrictions on U.S. government employees.

Michoacán state – Level 4: Do Not Travel

Do not travel due to crime. U.S. government employees are prohibited from travel in Michoacán state, with the exception of Morelia and Lazaro Cardenas cities and the area north of federal toll road 15D.

U.S. government employees are prohibited from travel by land, except on federal toll road 15D.

U.S. government employees may fly into Morelia and Lazaro Cardenas.

Visit our website for Travel to High-Risk Areas.

Morelos state – Level 3: Reconsider Travel

Reconsider travel due to crime. Violent crime and gang activity are common in parts of Morelos state.

U.S. government employees are prohibited from travel on any roads from Huitzilac to Santa Martha, Estado de Mexico, including Lagunas de Zempoala National Park and surrounding areas.

Visit our website for Travel to High-Risk Areas.

Nayarit state – Level 3: Reconsider Travel

Reconsider travel due to crime. Violent crime and gang activity are common in parts of Nayarit state.

U.S. government employees are prohibited from travel in most areas of the state, with the following exceptions:

- Santa Maria del Oro
- Xalisco

When traveling to permitted areas above, U.S. government employees must use major highways and cannot travel between cities after dark.

U.S. government employees are prohibited from patronizing adult clubs and gambling establishments in Nayarit.

Visit our website for Travel to High-Risk Areas.

Nuevo Leon state – Level 3: Reconsider Travel

Reconsider travel due to crime. Violent crime and gang activity are common in parts of Nuevo Leon state.

U.S. government employees may travel outside Monterrey only during daylight on toll roads, with the exception of travel to the Monterrey airport, which is permitted at any time.

U.S. government employees must remain within San Pedro Garza Garcia or Santa Catarina (south of the Santa Catarina river) municipalities between 1 a.m. and 6 a.m.

U.S. government employees are prohibited from patronizing adult clubs and gambling establishments in Nuevo Leon.

Visit our website for Travel to High-Risk Areas.

Oaxaca state – Level 2: Exercise Increased Caution

Exercise increased caution due to crime.

In Oaxaca, U.S. government employees are encouraged to remain in tourist areas and are not permitted to use public transportation.

U.S. government employees are prohibited from travel on Highway 200 throughout the state, except to transit between the airport in Huatulco to hotels in Puerto Escondido and Huatulco.

U.S. government employees are prohibited from travel to the El Istmo region. The El Istmo region is defined by Highway 185D to the west, Highway 190 to the north, and the Oaxaca/Chiapas border to the east and includes the towns of Juchitan de Zaragoza, Salina Cruz, and San Blas.

Puebla state – Level 2: Exercise Increased Caution

Exercise increased caution due to crime.

There are no travel restrictions on U.S. government employees.

Queretaro state – Level 2: Exercise Increased Caution

Exercise increased caution due to crime.

There are no travel restrictions on U.S. government employees.

Quintana Roo state – Level 2: Exercise Increased Caution

Exercise increased caution due to crime.

According to Government of Mexico statistics, the state experienced an increase in homicide rates compared to the same period in 2016. While most killing bystanders have occurred.

There are no restrictions on U.S. government employees for travel in Quintana Roo state, which includes tourist areas such as: Cancun, Cozumel, Playa del Carmen, Tulum, and the Riviera Maya.

San Luis Potosi state – Level 3: Reconsider Travel

Reconsider travel due to crime. Violent crime and gang activity are common in parts of San Luis Potosi state.

U.S. government employees may travel outside San Luis Potosi city only during daylight hours on toll roads. U.S. government employees must remain within San Luis Potosi city between 1 a.m. and 6 a.m.

U.S. government employees are prohibited from patronizing adult clubs and gambling establishments in San Luis Potosi.

Visit our website for Travel to High-Risk Areas.

Sinaloa state – Level 4: Do Not Travel

Do not travel due to crime. Violent crime is widespread. Criminal organizations are based and operating in Sinaloa state.

U.S. government employees are prohibited from travel in most areas of the state. In areas where travel is permitted, the following restrictions are in place:

- **Mazatlan:** U.S. government travel is permitted only in Zona Dorada, the historic town center, and direct routes to and from these locations and the airport or the cruise ship terminal.
- **Los Mochis and Port Topolobampo:** U.S. government travel is permitted within the city and the port, as well as direct routes to and from these locations and the airport.

Visit our website for Travel to High-Risk Areas.

Sonora state – Level 3: Reconsider Travel

Reconsider travel due to crime. Sonora is a key location used by the international drug trade and human trafficking networks. However, northern Sonora experiences much lower levels of crime than cities closer to Sinaloa and other parts of Mexico. U.S. government employees visiting Puerto Peñasco may use the Lukeville/Sonoyta crossing, and are required to travel during daylight hours on Route 8. U.S. government employees may also travel to Puerto Peñasco from Nogales by using Route 15 south and east via Routes 2 and 37 through Caborca during daylight hours. U.S. government employees may travel between the cities of Nogales and Hermosillo, however, travel is restricted to daylight hours and only on Route 15 through Imuris, Magdalena, and Santa Ana.

U.S. government employees are prohibited from travel to:

- The triangular region west of the Mariposa port-of-entry, east of Sonoyta, and north of Altar.
- The district within Nogales that lies to the north of Avenida Instituto Tecnologico and between Periferico and Corredor Fiscal, and the residential areas to the east of Plutarco Elias Calles. U.S. government employees are not permitted to use taxi services in Nogales, but bus travel is permitted. Movement around the city

- The eastern edge of the state of Sonora, which borders the state of Chihuahua (all points along that border east of Federal Highway 17, the road between Moctezuma and Sahuaripa, and state Highway 20 between Sahuaripa and the intersection with Federal Highway 16).
- South of Hermosillo, with the exception of the cities of Alamos, San Carlos, Guaymas, and Empalme.

Travel of U.S. government employees to the following cities is permitted with the noted restrictions:

- **San Luis Rio Colorado:** U.S. government employees must travel during daylight hours through the San Luis, Arizona port-of-entry and may not travel beyond the city limits.
- **Cananea:** U.S. government employees must travel during daylight hours through the Naco, Arizona port-of-entry and along Route 2 to Cananea, including the Cananea mine, and may not travel beyond the city limits.
- **Agua Prieta:** U.S. government employees must travel during daylight hours through the Douglas, Arizona port-of-entry and may not travel beyond the city limits.

Visit our website for Travel to High-Risk Areas.

Tabasco state – Level 2: Exercise Increased Caution

Exercise increased caution due to crime.

There are no travel restrictions on U.S. government employees.

Tamaulipas state – Level 4: Do Not Travel

Do not travel due to crime. Violent crime, such as murder, armed robbery, carjacking, kidnapping, extortion, and sexual assault, is common. Gang activity, including gun battles, is widespread. Armed criminal groups target public and private passenger buses traveling through Tamaulipas, often taking passengers hostage and demanding ransom payments. Local law enforcement has limited capability to respond to violence in many parts of the state.

U.S. government employees are subject to movement restrictions and a curfew between midnight and 6 a.m.

U.S. government employees are prohibited from patronizing adult clubs and gambling establishments in Tamaulipas.

Visit our website for Travel to High-Risk Areas.

Tlaxcala state – Level 2: Exercise Increased Caution

Exercise increased caution due to crime.

There are no travel restrictions on U.S. government employees.

Veracruz state – Level 2: Exercise Increased Caution

Exercise increased caution due to crime.

U.S. government employees are encouraged to remain in tourist areas and are not permitted to use public transportation. U.S. government employees are permitted to drive during daylight only.

Exercise increased caution. Police presence and emergency response are extremely limited outside of the state capital.

There are no restrictions on U.S. government employees for travel in Yucatan state, which includes tourist areas such as: **Chichen Itza, Merida, Uxmal,** and **Valladolid**.

Zacatecas state – Level 3: Reconsider Travel

Reconsider travel due to crime. Violent crime and gang activity are common in parts of Zacatecas state.

U.S. government employees may travel outside Zacatecas city only during daylight hours on toll roads. U.S. government employees must remain within Zacatecas city between 1 a.m. and 6 a.m.

U.S. government employees are prohibited from patronizing adult clubs and gambling establishments in Zacatecas.

Visit our website for Travel to High-Risk Areas.

Exhibit '13'

U.S. Department of State – Mexico: Secretary for Civilian Security, Democracy and Human Rights

U.S. Department of State
Diplomacy in Action

Mexico

Challenges

The success of the Government of Mexico's anti-drug, anti-organized crime and border security efforts remains critical to the U.S. Government's pursuit of its national drug control strategy and border security initiatives. With a 2,000-mile long land border with the United States and the largest volume of cross-border traffic in the world, Mexico is a major trans-shipment point for drugs and other contraband destined for the United States and Canada. Even with Mexico's continuing efforts to decrease illicit cultivation, Mexico remains one of the principal producers of heroin and marijuana destined for the United States. In 2014, the Government of Mexico seized over 3.6 metric tons (MT) of cocaine, 929.4 MT of marijuana, 424.5 kilograms (kg) of heroin, more than 19.8 MT of methamphetamine, and 1.4 MT of opium gum, and dismantled 143 methamphetamine labs. In 2013 and 2014 combined Mexico also reported seizures of 2,377 liters (L) of liquid forms of cocaine and 1,580 L of opium gum. Mexico-based transnational criminal organizations (TCOs) control drug trafficking to and within the United States. These TCOs are a source of considerable violence, corruption, and crime, including along the U.S.-Mexico border. In 2014, Mexico arrested several high profile traffickers and extradited 66 people to the United States to face charges related to drug trafficking and other crimes.

Merida Initiative Goals

Through the Merida Initiative, the United States and Mexico have engaged in an unprecedented partnership to break the power and impunity of transnational criminal organizations. Merida assistance helps strengthen border, air, and maritime controls; expand the capabilities and professionalization of Mexican law enforcement at the federal, state, and local levels; and improve the capacity to investigate and prosecute cases while transitioning to a new criminal justice system. The two countries also collaborate to bolster human rights and the rule of law, increase citizen security, and reduce the demand for drugs. Based on principles of shared responsibility, mutual trust, and respect for sovereign independence, these joint efforts have built confidence that has improved bilateral relationship.

The Strategic Framework for implementing the myriad of Merida Initiative activities and programs falls under Four Pillars. Each pillar pulls together Merida Initiative programs under the following strategic objectives:

Disrupt the Capacity of Organized Crime to Operate;
Institutionalize the Capacity to Sustain the Rule of Law;
Create a 21st century border; and
Build Strong and Resilient Communities.

Accomplishments

Since the Merida Initiative began in Fiscal Year 2008, the United States has provided Mexico with training, technical assistance, equipment, and "best practices" exchanges, including:

Delivery of aircraft that provide rapid transportation for law enforcement personnel, expanding Mexico's air mobility in counter narcotics and other security operations.

Ju

prosecutors, public defenders, investigators, and forensic experts.

Training for the Federal Police as well as state and local police, to assist in the strengthening and professionalization of Mexican law enforcement. Police professionalization efforts through the Merida Initiative support: (1) enforceable career standards; (2) pre-employment and periodic vetting and background investigations; (3) basic training through accreditation of police academies and addressing training deficiencies; (4) continuing education for law enforcement officials; (5) leadership and supervision; and (6) accountability, oversight, and integrity of police departments and active police officers.

Technical assistance, training, and equipment to the Mexican government to establish a corrections academy in the state of Veracruz, to train Mexico's federal correctional staff. With Merida assistance, the academy, nine federal prisons, nine state prisons, and the Chihuahua State Central Office for Prisons have received independent accreditation from the American Correctional Association (ACA). In addition, the ACA approved the initiation of an ACA Mexico Chapter. This chapter will help the Government of Mexico further their goals of achieving ACA accreditation in their prison system.

Scanners, x-ray machines, other non-intrusive inspection equipment, as well as over 400-trained canines, to enhance Mexican authorities' ability to detect and prevent the flow of illicit goods at key checkpoints and ports of entry along the border.

Help to establish joint intelligence task forces (JITFs) that now operate in four Mexican states. JITFs are comprised of carefully selected and vetted members of state and municipal police forces and state attorney general offices. The JITFs enable Mexican federal, state, and municipal law enforcement agencies to better share information, develop actionable intelligence, and foster greater inter-agency collaboration and coordination in LE operations.

Active support for the development and expansion of Mexico's first drug courts, which use treatment and community support as an alternative to incarceration. There are currently nine drug courts in operation in five Mexican states (Nuevo Leon, Chihuahua, Durango, State of Mexico, Morelos), with additional states under consideration.

Assistance for Mexico in creating a standardized certification program for drug treatment counselors. Beginning in 2012, 600 new counselors received training in a standardized curriculum developed with support from the Organization of American States' Inter-American Drug Abuse Control Commission. This program is in its second phase with a plan to train approximately 2,000 additional counselors.

Merida Initiative Culture of Lawfulness (COL) programs aim to instill a sense of individual responsibility to uphold the rule of law in Mexico, with the larger goal of reducing crime and corruption. COL programs supported the placement of citizens' watch booths in 73 local offices of the Mexico City district attorney, a program now also operating in Puebla and the State of Mexico. Citizens monitoring the booths provide information to people reporting crimes, advise them of their rights, and invite them to file criminal complaints, which has led to greater accountability and increased customer service in district attorneys' offices.

Exhibit '14'

Mexico 2018 Crime & Safety Report: Mexico City - OSAC

Report DETAILS

Attachments

Mexico Mexico City.pdf 261.89KB

Print Email

Mexico 2018 Crime & Safety Report: Mexico City

Travel Health and Safety; Transportation Security; Threats; Stolen items; Political Violence; Natural Disasters; Financial Security; Employee Health Safety; Intellectual Property Rights; Cyber; Crime; Cargo Security

Western Hemisphere > Mexico; Western Hemisphere > Mexico > Mexico City

3/9/2018

According to the current U.S. Department of State Travel Advisory at the date of this report's publication, Mexico has been assessed as Level 2: exercise increased caution.

Overall Crime and Safety Situation

U.S. Embassy Mexico City does not assume responsibility for the professional ability or integrity of the persons or firms appearing in this report. The ACS Unit cannot recommend a particular individual or location and assumes no responsibility for the quality of service provided.

The U.S. Department of State has assessed Mexico City as being a **CRITICAL**-threat location for crime directed at or affecting official U.S. government interests.

Please review OSAC's **Mexico-specific** webpage for original OSAC reporting, consular messages, and contact information, some of which may be available only to private-sector representatives with an OSAC password.

The Department of State divides its roles and responsibilities in Mexico among 10 consular districts. This Crime and Safety Report focuses on the Embassy's district, which is composed of Mexico City, the southern tip of Tamaulipas State and the following 13 states: Chiapas, Estado de México, Guanajuato, Guerrero, Hidalgo, Michoacán, Morelos, Oaxaca, Puebla, Querétaro, Tabasco, Tlaxcala, and Veracruz. For information regarding the security environment elsewhere, please reference the Crime and Safety Reports for Tijuana, Nogales, Hermosillo, Ciudad Juarez, Nuevo Laredo, Matamoros, Monterrey, Guadalajara, or Merida.

Crime Threats

The general crime rate in Mexico City is above the U.S. national average, and crime varies widely. The low rate of criminal convictions contributes to the high rate of crime. Although there is no pattern of criminals specifically targeting foreign or U.S. businesses/personnel, criminals will target anyone perceived as lucrative and vulnerable. Criminals select victims based on an appearance of prosperity, vulnerability, or a lack of awareness. Armed robberies, kidnappings, car thefts, credit card fraud, and various forms of residential/street crime are daily concerns. Jewelry (including expensive watches) and cellular phones can be sold are common crimes. Although Mexico employs strict gun-control laws, criminals are often armed with handguns or knives.

Organized criminal groups continue to cause significant levels of violence throughout parts of the country. The northern half of Mexico was considered a higher threat area, primarily due to organized criminal conflicts and competition for drug trafficking routes to the U.S.; however, recent statistics show that violence is on the rise in central and southern states, particularly in Guerrero, Michoacán, and Estado de México. One common practice is for gangs to charge protection fees or add their own tax to products/services with the threat of violence for those who fail to pay. Foreign and U.S. companies have been extorted, and some have been attacked for not responding to demands. Some criminal groups will mandate that individuals or even whole communities work for them as lookouts or couriers. Others will threaten municipal and state administrators into accepting corrupt practices. Beheadings, lynching, torture, and other gruesome displays of violence, as well as high numbers of forced disappearances, have become routine occurrences, including in the Mexico City metropolitan area. Numerous journalists and bloggers have been killed for reporting on these incidents.

Mexico is experiencing a combination of conditions that collectively degrade the security environment in certain areas. The government has captured some of its most wanted criminals. Consequently, organized criminal groups are becoming much less organized and disciplined. Various groups have splintered into smaller gangs, which have branched out into different illegal business activities, and associated violence is spreading across Mexico.

Cargo theft remains a key area of concern for U.S. and foreign companies. FreightWatch International ranks the level of cargo crime in Mexico as "severe," its worst ranking, primarily because the supply chain continues to face threats from cargo criminals, corrupt law enforcement personnel, and, to a smaller extent, organized crime. Mexico's Secretariat of Government estimates there were 7,286 cargo thefts in 2017, and FreightWatch has determined that cargo theft increased by roughly 19% compared with 2016 levels. Insurance policies have, therefore, experienced a cost increase, and some no longer provide coverage to overnight cargo travel.

There are numerous reports in which U.S. citizens have had their credit/debit card numbers skimmed and the money in their debit accounts stolen or their credit cards fraudulently charged. Skimming is the theft of credit card information by an employee of a legitimate merchant or bank, manually copying down numbers or using a magnetic stripe reader or using a camera and skimmer installed in an ATM. In addition to skimming, the risk of physical theft of credit or debit cards also exists. Try to use ATMs in bank branches during business hours. For more information, please review OSAC's Report, "**The Overseas Traveler's Guide to ATM Skimmers & Fraud.**"

Other Areas of Concern

According to the Procuraduria General de Justicia del Distrito Federal and the Secretaria Publica del Distrito Federal, the following city boroughs had the highest number of crimes reported in 2017: Cuauhtémoc, Iztapalapa, Gustavo A. Madero, Álvaro Obregón Venustiano Carranza and Coyoacan.

Travel for U.S. government employees is closely scrutinized due to violence associated with organized criminal groups. For a state-by-state assessment, visit the latest **U.S. Department of State Travel Advisory for Mexico**. The Embassy prohibits U.S. government employees' travel to several parts of the Embassy's district, including Guerrero and Michoacán.

Transportation-Safety Situation

For more information, please review OSAC's Report, "**Security in Transit: Airplanes, Public Transport, and Overnights.**"

Road Safety and Road Conditions

U.S. citizens traveling on roads and highways may encounter government checkpoints, which are often staffed by military personnel. The government has deployed federal police motorists who fail to stop at them. Likewise, self-defense groups have established checkpoints in their communities and have shot and wounded travelers who fail to stop. When approaching a checkpoint, regardless of whether it is official or non-official, cooperate and avoid any actions that may be perceived to be suspicious or aggressive.

For more information on self-driving, please review OSAC's Report "**Driving Overseas: Best Practices.**"

Public Transportation Conditions

The Embassy does not recommend using *libre* taxis, as they are poorly regulated and are often criminally-linked enterprises that pick up fares on the street after being hailed by customers. *Sitio* (radio-dispatched) taxis are far safer, more reliable, and are worth the added expense. These types of taxis cannot be hailed off the street and must be ordered by phone or met at a designated taxi stand. Twenty-four hour radio taxi service is available at 5516-6020 and 3626-9800 to 30. *Sitio* taxis in Mexico City are most often metered and registered by the government. In addition, the Embassy permits car services that can be requested online via phone/tablet applications, which allow consumers to verify the driver and vehicle number. For more information on ride-sharing, please review OSAC's Annual Briefing Report "**Safety and Security in the Share Economy.**"

Visitors should travel by intercity bus only during daylight hours and only by first-class conveyance whenever possible. Although there have been several reports of bus hijackings and robberies on toll roads, buses on toll roads have experienced a lower rate of incidents than second- and third-class buses that travel on less secure, *libre* highways.

There have been occasional reports of significant security incidents (apart from theft) on tourist buses in/around Mexico City and to nearby tourist destinations.

In Mexico City, municipal buses and the Metro (subway) are generally safe to use. City buses and the Metro may be crowded, and passengers should be on the alert for pickpockets and other thieves, especially on the most crowded, busiest routes during rush hour. Non-municipal buses (*micros*) are not well regulated and are not recommended.

Aviation/Airport Conditions

The Embassy advises that its employees fly, rather than drive, to many Mexican destinations.

Sitio taxis from Benito Juarez International Airport are paid in advance in the terminal (at the *sitio* stands) and are well-regulated.

Terrorism Threat

The U.S. Department of State has assessed Mexico City as being a **LOW**-threat location for terrorist activity directed at or affecting official U.S. government interests.

Local, Regional, and International Terrorism Threats/Concerns

The U.S. Embassy/Consulates are focused on Mexico as a potential transit country for foreign terrorist groups to conduct operations against the U.S. There are no known foreign terrorist organizations operating in Mexico, and there is no evidence that any terrorist group has targeted U.S. citizens in Mexico. Mexico does not provide a safe haven to terrorists or terrorist groups.

The Mexican government remained vigilant against domestic and foreign terrorist threats in 2017 and passed amendments to its Federal Penal Code that strengthened the country's legal framework to address acts of terrorism, including terrorist financing. Authorities cooperate well with relevant U.S. government agencies on persons of interest. Criminal organizations have used terror-like tactics (car bombs, grenades) to attack each other and security forces. They also commit gruesome acts of violence designed to terrorize; however, the effects of these acts seem directed largely at rival gangs.

The U.S. Department of State has assessed Mexico City as being a **HIGH**-threat location for political violence directed at or affecting official U.S. government interests.

Civil Unrest

Peaceful demonstrations of all sizes gather regularly at the Monument to Independence (the Angel), which is near the U.S. Embassy, to protest government policies, labor, social issues, and, occasionally, U.S. policies. These protests often affect traffic during peak commute hours on and near Paseo de La Reforma, the city's primary avenue. Most demonstrations are peaceful. However, even demonstrations intended to be peaceful may turn confrontational and escalate into violence. Demonstrators frequently block city streets, major highways, or take control of government toll roads on major highways and may demand unofficial tolls from travelers. Groups associated with teachers' unions and those protesting alleged human rights violations in Guerrero have used checkpoints as a way of raising money for their causes. U.S. citizens are urged to avoid areas of demonstrations and to exercise caution if in the vicinity of any protests.

Post-specific Concerns

Environmental Hazards

Earthquakes within the Embassy's consular district are routine, especially in the Pacific coast states. Mexico experienced an 8.2 earthquake on September 7, 2017, with epicenter off the coast of Oaxaca, and a 7.1 on September 19, 2017, with an epicenter in Morelos. Although there have been substantial improvements in building regulations and response planning since the 1985 earthquake, the 2017 earthquakes killed at least 441 people. Rebuilding costs are expected to exceed U.S.$1.6 billion.

Active and dormant volcanoes are scattered throughout central Mexico. One of the country's largest volcanoes, Popocatepetl, is located 43 miles southeast of Mexico City and has had several low-level eruptions in the past several years. The government prevents access to the mountain and has closed it to climbers and hikers. According to public safety officials, travelers to the area should have N-95 filter masks available in case ash falls on them. Clouds of ash associated with volcanic activity can limit air travel and make evacuation by air difficult.

- On November 23, 2017, Popocatepetl presented eruptive activity, which was considered the largest since 2013.

- On October 5, 2017, authorities raised the volcano alert system to "Yellow Phase 2" following an impressive eruption from Popocatepetl.

From May to November, hurricanes may affect the Pacific and Gulf coasts of the Embassy's consular district. The coastal states tend to bear the brunt of these storms, but storms have caused flooding and disruption of utility services throughout the district. During September 2017, three hurricanes hit Mexico's coasts:

- Katia (Category 1, hit Veracruz shore on September 8)

- Lidia (Category 1, hit Baja California's Peninsula on September 1)

- Max (Category 1, hit Guerrero's shores on September 14)

Critical Infrastructure

On July 18, 2017, rains caused thousands of gallons of *jales* (water contaminated with waste from the mining extraction process) to spill onto farm lands and water streams in the

- October 16: X-ray equipment containing Iridium 192 was stolen from a parked vehicle in Nayarit.

- August 1: A nuclear densimeter was stolen from an Universidad de Nuevo Leon vehicle in Nuevo Leon.

- April 25: An ambulance containing iridium 192 (a radioactive material) was stolen in Jalisco.

In 2017, the Ministry of Labor (Secretaria del Trabajo y Prevision Social, STPS) and Institute of Social Security (Instituto Mexicano del Seguro Social, IMSS) reported 158,808 (closed) cases of industrial and transportation accidents, including work illnesses.

Economic Concerns

Mexico was listed on the Watch List in the **2017 Special 301 Report**, noting inadequate intellectual property rights (IPR) enforcement and the wide availability of pirated/counterfeit goods, mostly via physical and virtual markets. Criminal organizations are significantly involved in the counterfeit and pirated goods trade. Enforcement efforts suffer from weak coordination among federal, state, and municipal officials; limited resources for prosecutions; lack of long-term sustained investigations to target high-level suppliers; and the need for deterrent level penalties. The U.S. continues to encourage Mexico to provide its customs officials with *ex-officio* authority, to allow the Attorney General Offices the authority to prosecute transshipments of alleged counterfeit and pirated goods, and to enact legislation to strengthen its copyright regime, including the World Intellectual Property Organization (WIPO) Internet Treaties. The U.S. also continues to work with Mexico to resolve IPR concerns through bilateral, regional, and other means of engagement.

Economic espionage activity is covered under misappropriation of trade secrets law in Mexico. The three sources of trade secrets law are the Industrial Property Law, Federal Criminal Code, and NAFTA, all of which provide fines and criminal penalties for misappropriation of trade secrets. There have been extremely limited prosecutions of trade secret misappropriation due to onerous legal requirements and evidentiary issues tied to proving theft of digital files.

Kidnapping Threat

The number of kidnappings reported throughout Mexico is of particular concern. The number of kidnapping incidents is difficult to determine because most of the cases are not reported to authorities, as the popular belief is that the police may be involved or are unable to resolve the situation.

The majority of cases reported to the U.S. Embassy have been kidnapping for ransom (KFR) cases. In some KFR cases, a ransom is paid, and the victim set free, but in other cases, the victims are killed despite having paid a ransom. Affluent residents in Mexico City often have bodyguards and armored vehicles for their families.

While kidnappings can occur anywhere, government of Mexico statistics state that 771 kidnapping cases were reported within Embassy Mexico City's consular district in 2017. States within the consular district with the highest number of kidnappings in 2017 were Estado de México, Veracruz, Guerrero, and Tabasco, representing a 3% decrease compared to 2016 statistics. Police (or former law enforcement officials) have been implicated in many of these incidents.

The FBI investigated 116 kidnapping events in Mexico in 2017. In 66 of them, the victim was a U.S. citizen, in 14 the victim was a Legal Permanent Resident, and in 36 cases the extortion/ransom call was placed to a number in the U.S. Of the cases, 81 were kidnappings for ransom, 25 were virtual kidnappings, and in 10 cases there was no ransom demand. Travelers are advised to vary routes/times and to be alert to possible surveillance, noting any individual who appears out of place. When hiring domestic help, vet them by identifying

The number of reported express kidnappings is low. Express kidnappings are based on the 24-hour withdrawal limit placed on ATM cards industry-wide. Express kidnapping victims are held for 24-48 hours to maximize withdrawal amounts. A common *modus operandi* for express kidnappings in Mexico City is passengers using *libre* taxis who are often robbed by two or three armed accomplices who enter the taxi a few minutes into the trip. The term 'express kidnapping' is also applied to the kidnapping of random victims held for brief periods where only small ransom amounts are demanded. A typical scenario may last for several hours and may be settled for the peso-equivalent of a few hundred or thousand dollars. Few official U.S. government employees have suffered this type of crime, but many Mexican employees of the Embassy either have been victimized themselves or know a victim.

There appears to be an up-tick in virtual kidnappings. These extortion telephone calls vary in style, but the methodology is often the same. Callers say that they have kidnapped a loved one and often include a crying/pleading voice immediately after the call is answered but before the kidnapper gets on the phone. Callers intend to confuse the victim and trick them into giving away important information. The voice will usually be crying and/or hysterical, making it difficult to identify and increasing the likelihood that the victim will believe it is their loved one. Criminals use fear and timing against victims. They plan their calls to coincide with times when it is difficult to contact the victim (when children are on their way to/from school). Or, the callers will obtain two cell phones of two family members. They will call both victims at the same time and claim to have kidnapped the other. They use fear and the threat of violence to keep both victims on the line while they urge them to pay a ransom. Once the kidnappers are satisfied they have obtained as much money as they can, they end the call. They may demand that the ransom be delivered in person, which can turn into a real kidnapping, or that the money is sent electronically. Variations use callers claiming to be lawyers or police looking to get a family member out a bad situation. They pressure the target to pay them to waive charges or to bribe alleged corrupt officials to free their loved one and avoid a long, expensive judicial process.

Virtual kidnapping/extortion calls are made to Mexican and international numbers and often use information obtained from social networking websites. A variation affecting travelers at hotels is an extortion-by-deception scheme, wherein a victim is called and convinced to isolate themselves from family/friends until a ransom is paid. The victim is coerced (by threat of violence) to remain isolated and to provide phone numbers for the victim's family/loved ones. The victim's family is contacted, and a ransom is extracted. Often, the callers make statements to suggest surveillance.

To reduce the likelihood of receiving a virtual kidnapping call, answer the phone with only a "hello" and make the other person ask for you by name and know the details of your family's itinerary and contact information (land-line and cell phone numbers). Never provide personal information to someone who calls or approaches you and do not post personal information on social networking sites.

For more information, please review OSAC's Report, "**Kidnapping: The Basics.**"

Police Response

The government of Mexico has deployed security forces to various parts of the country and has created a new military unit known as the National Gendarmerie to augment security in certain areas.

Be aware that offering a bribe to a public official to avoid a ticket or other penalty is a crime. U.S. citizens are advised to cooperate with the police if stopped or questioned.

How to Handle Incidents of Police Detention or Harassment

In some instances, U.S. citizens have become victims of harassment, mistreatment, or extortion by law enforcement and other officials. Authorities have cooperated in investigating some cases, but one must have the officer's name, badge number, and patrol car number to pursue a complaint effectively. U.S. citizens are advised to note this information if they have a problem with police or other officials.

U.S. citizens may contact the Consular Section at the U.S. Embassy in Mexico City for assistance in dealing with the police. If involved in a traffic accident or victimized by crime, one may be required to accompany the investigating officer to the local police station to file a complaint or respond to questions. Should a police report be required for an insurance claim, a nominal fee will be charged.

Host Nation Police Emergency: 911

Fire Department: 911

Ambulance: 911 (Red Cross)

Consejo Ciudadano de Seguridad Publica y Procuracion de Justicia del Distrito Federal (in Mexico City, takes complaints from those afraid to go to the police): 5533-5533

Police/Security Agencies

Procuraduria General de la Republica (PGR): Office of the Mexican Attorney General that is responsible for investigating and prosecuting federal crimes.

Secretary of Interior (Secretaría de Gobernación, SEGOB): Oversees federal police forces. The federal police are approximately 38,000 strong and are present in all states. They oversee the Mexican Immigration Service (INAMI), whose officers have the right to detain suspected undocumented aliens and may deport them without formal deportation proceedings.

Secretariat of Finance and Public Credit (Secretaría de Hacienda y Crédito Público): Customs officers (Aduana) are deployed at borders and at international airports to interdict contraband.

The Bank of Mexico (Banco de México): Operates its own security division, which is charged with enforcing banking and monetary laws, including cases of counterfeiting, fraud, and money laundering.

Procuraduria General de Justicia (PGJ): The local Mexican Attorney in each state/city is in charge of investigating and prosecuting state and local crimes.

State Police: Each of the country's 31 states and the Federal District maintain both preventive and judicial police. State police are under the direction of the state's governor.

Municipal Police: Each state contains numerous municipalities, each of which maintains a municipal police force.

Military Forces: The army and navy have been heavily involved in anti-crime initiatives, as they combat organized criminal groups.

Medical Emergencies

Useful information on medical emergencies abroad, including overseas insurance programs, is provided Consular Affairs' website Your Health Abroad.

Contact Information for Recommended Hospitals/Clinics

For medical assistance, please refer to the Embassy's Medical Assistance page.

Available Air Ambulance Services

Advanced Air Ambulance 800-633-3590 or 305-232-7700

Air Ambulance Professionals 800-752-4195 or 954-730-9300

Recommended Insurance Posture

Exhibit '15'

<u>'The Borgen Project'</u> the Blog, Top Diseases in Mexico: Symptoms Prevalence & Treatment, October 2016

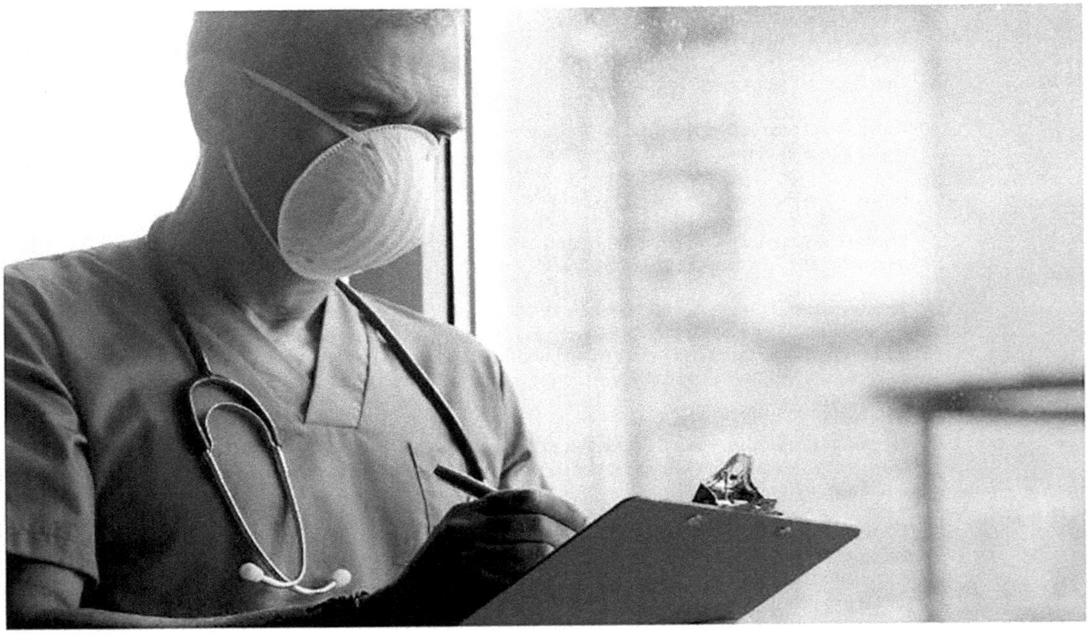

THE BORGEN PROJECT

- About

- Issues

- Act Now

- The Blog
- Magazine
- Be a Donor

An influential ally for the world's poor.

- Facebook
- Twitter

search site

The Blog

You are here: Home » The Blog » The Blog » Global health » Top Diseases in Mexico: Symptoms, Prevalence & Treatment

October 3, 2016
03 Oct 2016

Top Diseases in Mexico: Symptoms, Prevalence & Treatment

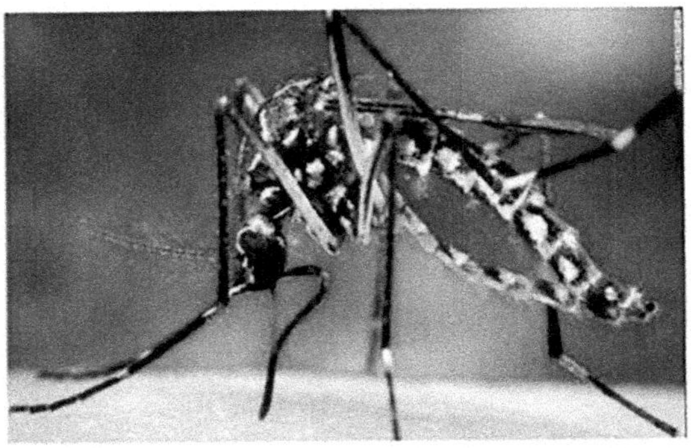

Diseases can prove very hard to prevent, control, and treat; and, many countries suffer from maladies that cannot be tamed. Mexico is no exception, and the top diseases in Mexico can inflict a great deal of damage. A summarization of each disease can be found below, including details on how the illness is transmitted and treated, the symptoms, and prevention tactics.

Top Diseases in Mexico

1. **Hepatitis A**
   Hepatitis A can be spread via contaminated food or water or spread through person-to-person contact. A person to person transmission can occur when an infected person's stool is ingested by a non-infected person through poor hygiene practices. Poor hygiene and sanitation practices are the results of letting half the country's population live in abject poverty; without clean drinking water or sewage services, Hepatitis A spreads easily and is now endemic to the population of Mexico. To clarify, if a disease is endemic that means the illness is regularly found among a population; for Mexico, Hepatitis A is found throughout the entire country.
2. **Dengue Virus**
   This virus is transmitted by mosquitos. Symptoms at the beginning of incubation of the virus includes a sudden high fever, joint pain and headaches. Dengue is endemic to all of Mexico as well, except for the state of Baja California Norte and other areas of higher elevation because mosquitoes carrying the virus cannot survive at the higher elevations. Dengue may progress into dengue shock syndrome, a rare complication including a hemorrhagic fever, damage to lymph and blood vessels, bleeding from the nose and gums, enlargement of the liver, and even failure of the circulatory system, which can cause death. Taking aspirin accelerates the onset of symptoms of dengue shock syndrome, as aspirin thins the blood, so it is important to quickly ascertain that dengue is causing a patient's symptoms before administering medication. Protection against contracting the dengue virus is easy: use bug spray, wear layers outdoors, and make sure bug screens in the home have no holes or tears for mosquitoes to fly through. Although seemingly simple, these precautions are monumental tasks for the poor of Mexico, who struggle to provide food for their families, let alone mosquito repellant.

Elevating the Impoverished

Diseases transmitted by mosquitoes are more likely to disproportionately affect those in lower economic classes. The Baker Institute mentions that these diseases, also known as neglected tropical diseases (NTDs), are widespread in Mexico's poorest southern states such as Chiapas, Oaxaca, Guerrero, and Mayan villages on the outskirts of the Yucatan Peninsula.

Elevating the status and resource access of the impoverished in Mexico is an absolutely essential measure to alleviating the top diseases in Mexico.

Exhibit '16'

Copy of the Police Incident Report of the Applicant

Incident Report

OAKLAND POLICE DEPARTMENT

Incident Summary

Incident Type: ROBBERY
Report Type: INCIDENT REPORT
Inc Occurred Address: 102ND AV & BANCROFT AV, OAKLAND, CALIFORNIA
Sector/Beat: CCD7/32Y
Inc Occurred Start: 01/27/2018 22:14 Inc Occurred End: 01/27/2018 22:14
Report Taken:
Bias Motivation: Gang Related: N
Substance: U
Contact Nature: NO
Reported Date/Time: 01/27/2018 22:20
Reporting Officer: MINOR, DESIREE
Primary Assigned Officer: HAYNES, SAMANTHA
Case Status: INVESTIGATOR CL Disposition: FILE PENDING
Disposition Date: 02/06/2018 13:54

Offenses

Statute Code: PC211 Enhancers: ARM
Statute Desc: ROBBERY-FIREARM
Counts: 2 Statute Severity: Felony

Statute Code: PC242 Enhancers:
Statute Desc: BATTERY
Counts: 2 Statute Severity: Misdemeanor

Statute Code: PC273 A(B) Enhancers:
Statute Desc: WILLFUL CRUELTY TO CHILD
Counts: 1 Statute Severity: Misdemeanor

Officers

Event Association	Emp#	Badge#	Name	Squad#
REPORTING OFFICER	9476		MINOR, DESIREE	
Primary Responding Officer	9476		MINOR, DESIREE	
REPORTING OFFICER'S SUPERVIS	8630		COGLIO, RICHARD	
REVIEWER	8630		COGLIO, RICHARD	
PRIMARY ASSIGNED OFFICER	4766		HAYNES, SAMANTHA	

Persons Involved

Person#: 0001
Event Association: VICTIM
Name:
Age: 24 - 24

Address: 533 3RD AV, SAN BRUNO, CALIFORNIA 94066
Sector/Beat: /99X

Incident Report

OAKLAND POLICE DEPARTMENT

Property Involved

Property # 0001 | Evidence: No

Event Assoc/Orig status: STOLEN | Original Status Date: | Original Value:

Current Status: STOLEN | Current Status Date: 1/26/2018 22:14:00 | Current Value:

Property Type:

Description: ONE(1) BROWN PURSE, CONTAINING VICTIM ID AND DEBIT CARD

Make/Brand: UNKNOWN | Model: UNKNOWN

Color: BROWN | Quantity: 1

Serial/Lot#: | Owner Applied#:

NCIC Date: | NCIC Reported By:

NCIC#: | NCIC Cancelled:

Property # 0002 | Evidence: No

Event Assoc/Orig status: STOLEN | Original Status Date: 1/27/2018 22:14:00 | Original Value: $1,200.00

Current Status: STOLEN | Current Status Date: 1/27/2018 22:14:00 | Current Value: $1,200.00

Property Type:

Description: TWO(2) CELLULAR PHONE, APPLE, IPHONE 7, BLK

Make/Brand: APPLE | Model: IPHONE 7

Color: BLACK | Quantity: 2

Serial/Lot#: | Owner Applied#:

NCIC Date: | NCIC Reported By:

NCIC#: | NCIC Cancelled:

Property # 0003 | Evidence: No

Event Assoc/Orig status: STOLEN | Original Status Date: 1/27/2018 22:14:00 | Original Value: $400.00

Current Status: STOLEN | Current Status Date: 1/27/2018 22:14:00 | Current Value: $400.00

Property Type:

Description: ONE(1) APPLE, IWATCH 1 SERIES, BLK

Make/Brand: APPLE | Model: IWATCH, SERIES 1

Color: BLACK | Quantity: 1

Serial/Lot#: | Owner Applied#:

NCIC Date: | NCIC Reported By:

NCIC#: | NCIC Cancelled:

Incident Report

OAKLAND POLICE DEPARTMENT

Modus Operandi

Against Persons:
Against Property:
Occupied:
General Premise 1:
General Premise 2:
Specific Premise:
Surrounding Area 1:
Surrounding Area 2:
Surrounding Area 3:
Relationship to Suspect 1:
Relationship to Suspect 2:
Weapon Type 1:
Automatic:
Weapon Type 2:
Automatic:
Weapon Type 3:
Automatic:

Crime Against Property

of Premises Entered:
Entry Point:
Exit Point:
Entry Loc 1:
Exit Loc 1:
Entry Loc 2:
Exit Loc 2:
Entry Method 1:
Exit Method 1:
Entry Method 2:
Exit Method 2:
Entry Tool 1:
Exit Tool 1:
Entry Tool 2:
Exit Tool 2:
Vehicle Entry:
Safe Entry:

Suspect Action 1:
Suspect Action 2:
Suspect Action 3:
Suspect Action 4:
Suspect Action 5:
Additional Factor 1:
Additional Factor 2:
Additional Factor 3:
Additional Factor 4:
Additional Factor 5:
Security Type:
Victim Location:
Electronic Locks:
Video Surveillance:
Maid:
Inspectress:

Crime Against Persons

Pre-incident Contact 1:
Pre-incident Contact 2:
Pre-incident Contact 3:
Victim Condition 1:
Victim Condition 2:
Victim Condition 3:
Victim Condition 4:
Victim Condition 5:
Suspect Solicited 1:
Suspect Solicited 2:
Suspect Pretended to Be:

Suspect Action 1:
Suspect Action 2:
Suspect Action 3:
Suspect Action 4:
Suspect Action 5:
Sex Crime 1:
Sex Crime 2:
Sex Crime 3:
Sex Crime 4:
Sex Crime 5:
Vehicle Involvement 1:

Incident Report

Narratives

ENTERED DATE/TIME: 1/27/2018 22:20:00
SUBJECT: SYNOPSIS
AUTHOR: MINOR, DESIREE

PC211-ROBBERY FIREARM (X2)
PC242-BATTERY (X2)

Not I/C

ENTERED DATE/TIME: 1/27/2018 22:20:00
SUBJECT: FBR NARRATIVE
AUTHOR: MINOR, DESIREE

Suspect Ingress / Egress DOF - Ingress-Parked at 102nd Ave and Bancroft Av/ Egress EB Bancroft Ave toward San Leandro.

Victim Ingress / Egress DOF (Where were they coming from or what were they doing?) - Parked near 102nd Av and Bancroft Ave, walking to 2137 102nd Ave

Victim(s) email address - crystal.ponce650@gmail.com

Is the Cell Phone Traceable? No

Were Credit Cards Taken? Used? (Indicate date, time, location, amount charged, and last four numbers of CC) - Yes, unknown- canceled

Vehicle (Plate Description) - Hond, Accord, 4D, Blue

Video Available (Retrieved, Location, Quality, Contact Info if Not Recovered, Name, #, and Note video time sequence for ease of review) - N/A

Tech Tag Left - No

Identifiable Suspect - No

Suspects known to the neighborhood -Unknown

Weapon(s) Used - Handgun

Incident Report

OAKLAND POLICE DEPARTMENT

Log Entry / DNR Made - Yes

~~LOSS:~~

1) One(1) Brown Purse, Containing Victim ID And Debit Card
2) Two(2) Cellular Phone, Apple, Iphone 7, Blk, valued at $1200 USD
3) One(1) Apple, Iwatch 1 Series, 42 inch, Blk, valued at $400 USD

SUMMARY:

On 27 Jan 18, at about 2214 hrs, I was working as OPD Patrol Unit 3L32. I was wearing full OPD Utility uniform and driving fully marked patrol crown victoria #1731. Radio dispatched me to 2137 102rd Ave to investigate the report of a robbery.

Upon arrival, I contacted [redacted] and [redacted] I observed [redacted] had blood on her lip. I observed [redacted] had swelling to the right side of his face. [redacted] and [redacted] advised they had just been robbed. I ordered medical to the scene to evaluation [redacted] and [redacted]

With the information [redacted] provided, I conducted a crime broadcast providing Officers in the area with the suspect descriptions, direction of flight and the loss items.

I took a PDRD statement from [redacted] stated the following, but not verbatim:

On 27 Jan 18, at about 2214 hrs, [redacted] was walking with her husband, [redacted] and [redacted] from their vehicle parked at 102nd Ave and Bancroft Ave to their relatives' residence at [redacted] 102nd Ave. [redacted] were approached by S-1 and S-2 who exited VEH1(Hond, Acc, 4D Blue) which was parked in front of them. S-1 presented a black handgun, hit PONCE in the mouth with his closed fist, while she was holding [redacted] and demanded [redacted] belongings. Fearing for her safety and [redacted] safety, [redacted] handed her purse(containing her ID, a debit card and her Iphone 7) to S-1. S-1 and S-2 then approached [redacted] and started to kick and hit him several times, causing him to fall to the ground. S-1 and S-2 fled the scene with the loss in VEH1 driving EB on Bancroft Ave. PONCE can identity S-1 and S-1 if she saw them again. [redacted] wants to press charges and will assist with the prosecution. See PDRD statement for further.

Ofc. S. Kofford 9470P took a PDRD statement from [redacted] who advised the following, but not verbatim:

Incident Report

OAKLAND POLICE DEPARTMENT

Ave, when they were approached by S-1 and S-2. observed S-1 approach and hit her in the face, while she was holding their S-1 and S-2 then approached and started to hit and kick him several times, while yelling . Fearing for his safety, ~~CAMPOS TRUJILLO took off his watch(loss item#3), removed his iphone7 from his pocket and threw them to the suspects. S-1 and S-2 kicked a few more times, before running back to VEH1. S-1 and S-2~~ then fled the scene with the loss items in VEH1, driving EB on Bancroft Ave. did not observe the firearm. wants to press charges and will assist with the prosecution. See PDRD statement for further.

were provided a blue card with their RD#, a resource card for victims of violent crimes and a Marsy's card.

were transported to Eden Hospital by PMP 2222 for further assessment.

I contacted the OPD Patrol Desk and submitted a DNR/Log Entry. I contacted OPD Service and submitted a Communications Order.

Based on preliminary investigation, it appears that on 27 Jan 18, at about 2214 hrs, were walking in the 2100 blk of 102nd Ave, when they were approached by S-1 and S-2. S1 presented a firearm and hit in the mouth with his fist(in violation of 242 PCX1), while was holding her S-1 demanded possessions (in violation of 211PCX1), fearing for her safety and the anded her purse (containing ID, debit card and Iphone) it to S-1(in Violation of 211PCx1). S-1 and S-2 then approached and started to kick and punch him several times(in violation of 242PCx1), demanding his belongings. Fearing for his safety, gave the suspects his iphone and iwatch (in violation of 211PCX1). S-1 and S-2 then fled EB on Bancroft Ave in VEH1 with the loss.

PDRD activated.

Incident Report

OAKLAND POLICE DEPARTMENT

No force was used or observed.

Exhibit '17'

Letter from Lt. Robert ROSIN to the Applicant's Spouse concerning the Investigation of the Applicant's ongoing case

CITY OF OAKLAND

POLICE ADMINISTRATION BUILDING • 455 – 7TH STREET 5

Police Department

Telephone Device for the Deaf (510) 238-3227
Patrol Desk (510) 238-3455
Fax (510) 238-2251

02/05/18

533 3rd Ave
San Bruno, CA 94066

RE: Criminal Investigation –

Dear: [redacted]

My name is Lieutenant Robert Rosin and I am the commander of the Felony Assault/Robbery and Burglary Section, I am writing to you in regards to your police report (Oakland Police Number

We understand the serious nature of your case and are committed to doing everything we can to investigate as many cases as possible. Due the totality of the circumstances, and the information we have available to us regarding this case, it does not warrant further investigation or presentation to the District Attorney's Office at this time. Your case is being filed pending additional evidentiary leads. If you have additional information regarding your case, or do not wish to pursue your case please call the Robbery Section at

Should you have any concerns or questions regarding this letter, please feel free to contact me.

Sincerely,

Robert Rosin
Lieutenant of Police
Robbery/Burglary

Exhibit '18'

Psychological Evaluation of the Applicant

July 7, 2018

RE: Psychological evaluation of Mr. ██████ ██████

This report is to provide you with my clinical assessment; progress formulation, mental status examination and treatment plan for the above-mentioned client.

IDENTIFYING INFORMATION

Mr. ██████ ██████ is a 28-year-old Latin male. He was born in Mexico and has been residing in the U.S.A. for the past 14 years. Mr. ██████ ██████ has been married to Mrs. Cristal Odalis Ponce Gutierrez, at 23 years of age, since December 25, 2016. They have three children together; ████████ █████ Ponce at 8 years of age, █████████ ██████ ████ at 6 years of age and █████████ █████ Ponce at 1 year of age. Mr. ██████ ██████ currently resides with his wife and three children.

VICTIM OF CRIME INCIDENT

Mr. ██████ ██████ stated, "This incident happened in January of 2018. We were at my cousin's house during the incident. While walking back to the car, we remembered that we forgot the keys so we got off to get the keys. I noticed a car where two tall men came out from. They came towards me and they began hitting me. They took away my cell phone and demanded to get all of my possessions. As I was being hit, I was handing over my stuff. They stole my wife's purse with her cell. My daughter was hugging my wife during this time. I ended up on the floor. I got up and didn't see my wife. I started walking towards my cousin's house and had bruises all over my face. We called the police and an investigation began but they still haven't found the guys. My two sons stayed at my cousin's house for a sleepover and my baby was the only witness. They hit my wife and since she was carrying my baby, my baby's lips began bleeding because her head accidentally hit my wife's head while my wife was giving up her purse. The ambulance took me to the hospital and it was just horrible!"

An investigation was conducted by the Oakland Police Department.

HOW LIFE HAS CHANGED SINCE THE INCIDENT

Mr. ████ ████ stated, "My life has changed drastically. I use to keep my dog in the backyard but now, I bring the dog in because I fear something bad might happen to my dog. I also lock my garage door and every door I enter whether it is in the car or my house. I feel more anxious than usual and can't sleep like I use to. I think I have insomnia. I feel like I lost confidence in myself. When I go somewhere, I always come back to the house like 3 more times to check if I locked everything; I was never like this before. When I walk, I am always looking behind me and near me to see who is around. I feel paranoid."

DIAGNOSIS

Mr. ████ ████ has been diagnosed with conditions labeled as Major Depressive Disorder, Recurrent and Severe without Psychotic Features, Generalized Anxiety Disorder and Post Traumatic Stress Disorder (PTSD) due to the frequency, intensity and duration of his symptoms. Mr. ████ ████ condition began when he was robbed. Mr. ████ ████ response to the event involved intense fear, helplessness and terror.

MAJOR DEPRESSIVE DISORDER

Major Depressive Disorder (MDD) is a disabling condition that adversely affects a person's family, work or school life and general health. In the United States, around 3.4% of people with major depression commit suicide, and up to 60% of people who commit suicide had depression or another mood disorder. The diagnosis of Major Depressive Disorder is based on the patient's self-reported experiences, behavior reported by relatives or friends and a mental status examination. There is no laboratory test for major depression, although physicians may request for testing that may cause similar symptoms. A major depressive episode is characterized by the presence of a severely depressed mood that persists for at least two weeks to a lifelong disorder with recurrent episodes. Episodes may be isolated or recurrent and are categorized as mild (few symptoms in excess of minimum criteria), moderate, or severe (marked impact on social or occupational functioning). An episode with psychotic features — commonly referred to as psychotic depression — is automatically rated as severe. Typically, patients are treated with antidepressant medication in conjunction to receiving outpatient mental health services or counseling. The need for hospitalization may be necessary if there is a significant risk of harm to self or others. Depressed individuals have shorter life expectancies than those without depression, due to their susceptibility to medical illnesses and suicide.

Mr. ████ ████ reported experiencing symptoms that are consistent with Major Depressive Disorder, Recurrent and Severe without Psychotic Features such as: (a) sadness and depressed mood (b) crying spells (c) irritability (d) feelings of guilt (e) loss of interest, energy and motivation (f) decrease of sleep and (g) nightmares with morbid themes (despair).

Mr. ████ ████ reported feeling sad and depressed. He stated, "I feel sad and depressed because I am not the same since the incident. I am especially sad when I think about the possible separation that my family may endure because I do not have my legal papers to stay in this country." Mr. ████ ████ reported having crying spells. He stated, "I cry but secretly, because I don't want my children to get afraid. I want to be a good dad and want the best for my children. I cry thinking that I may be taken to Mexico and be separated from my family as well." Mr. ████ ████ reported feeling irritable. He stated, "I feel irritated because I used to let my children have a little more freedom but now, I feel like I control their every move trying to protect them." Mr. ████ ████ reported having feelings of guilt. He stated, "I feel guilty because ever since the incident, I have become more over-protective of my family especially my children. I don't let them go out as often because I fear that something can happen to them. When I go places, I make sure to close the door and lock it whether it be in the car or home because I am afraid." Mr. ████ ████ reported having a loss of energy and motivation resulting to a loss of interest in previously enjoyed social or pleasurable activities. He stated, "I don't feel comfortable or motivated to be out anymore. I used to be out a lot and walk my dog, but now, I don't because of fear and lack of motivation." Mr. ████ ████ reported having a decrease of sleep. He stated, "I cannot sleep because I am so nervous that this will happen again." Mr. ████ ████ reported experiencing nightmares with morbid themes (despair). He stated, "I get nightmares often since the incident. I dream of people following me and I am unable to run. I have my children with me and try to protect them but cannot."

Mr. ████ ████ reported that he has been experiencing depressive symptoms for the past 6 months, on an intermittent basis, as a result of the assault he experienced. The above-mentioned symptoms hinder his ability to function with normal daily activities and maintain healthy and bonding relationships with others.

TREATMENT PLAN

Mr. ████ ████ treatment plan consists of teaching him adaptive self-coping skills, effective problem solving skills, and increasing his support system. It is recommended that Mr. ████ ████ receive outpatient mental health services on a monthly or as needed basis.

GENERALIZED ANXIETY DISORDER

Generalized Anxiety Disorder (GAD) is characterized by persistent, excessive, unrealistic, uncontrollable worry about everyday life activities. Individuals who suffer from this diagnosis anticipate disaster and are overly concerned about money, health, family, work, or other issues.

Generalized Anxiety Disorder is diagnosed when a person worries excessively about a variety of everyday problems for at least 6 months. Sometimes just the thought of getting through the day produces anxiety. Such individuals don't know how to stop the worry cycle and feel it is beyond their control, even though they usually realize that their anxiety is more intense than the situation warrants. Generalized Anxiety Disorder affects 6.8 million adults, or 3.1% of the U.S. population, in any given year. Women are twice as likely to be affected. The disorder comes on gradually and can begin across the life cycle, though the risk is highest between childhood and middle age. Although the exact cause of Generalized Anxiety Disorder is unknown, there is evidence that biological factors, family background, and life experiences, particularly stressful ones, play a role.

Mr. ████ ████ reported experiencing symptoms that are consistent with Generalized Anxiety Disorder such as: (a) excessive anxiety and worry (b) nervousness (c) restlessness (d) difficulty with concentration (e) headaches and **(f) panic attacks**

Mr. ████ ████ reported having excessive anxiety and worry. He stated, "I am worried about this happening again." Mr. ████ ████ reported feeling nervous. He stated, "I am very nervous and I bite my nails since the incident." Mr. ████ ████ reported feeling restless. He stated, "I feel restless and I am always moving around. Like at my house, I am always looking around and fidgeting." Mr. ████ ████ reported having difficulty with focus and concentration. He stated, "I can't focus or concentrate." Mr. ████ ████ reported having headaches. He stated, "I have headaches often because of the stress that my body carries." Mr. ████ ████ reported experiencing panic attacks. He stated, "I have started having panic attacks since the incident where I can't breathe and my body feels hot."

Mr. ████ ████ reported experiencing anxiety symptoms for the past 6 months, on an intermittent basis, as a result of the assault and trauma he experienced. Mr. ████ ████ symptoms hinder his ability to function with normal daily activities, such as trying to perform simple daily tasks. The intensity of his symptoms leads to thoughts of a foreshortened future, such as not expecting to have a healthy and normal lifestyle.

TREATMENT PLAN

Mr. ████ ████ treatment plan consists of various interventions aimed at helping him manage his anxiety symptoms. Self-relaxation techniques and thought stopping techniques have been introduced to help Mr. ████ ████ cope with his anxiety symptoms. It is recommended that Mr. ████ ████ receive outpatient mental health services on a monthly or as needed basis.

POST TRAUMATIC STRESS DISORDER

Post Traumatic Stress Disorder (PTSD) most commonly occurs when an individual is faced with a traumatic event that threatens their safety or makes them feel helpless, such as in Mr. ████ ████ case. However, any overwhelming life experience can trigger PTSD, especially if the event feels unpredictable and uncontrollable. Post Traumatic Stress Disorder (PTSD) can affect those who personally experience the catastrophe and those who witness it. The symptoms of PTSD most commonly develop in the hours or days following the traumatic event, or it can sometimes take weeks, months, or even years before they appear. The severity of the violence, the duration of exposure, early-age onset, and the victim's cognitive assessment of the violence (perceived degree of threat, predictability, and controllability) exacerbate the symptoms. The extent, severity, and type of abuse are associated with the intensity of PTSD.

Mr. ████ ████ reported symptoms that are consistent with Post Traumatic Stress Disorder, Chronic such as: (a) recurring distressing recollections or flashbacks of prior trauma events (b) intense psychological distress at exposure to triggers (c) efforts to avoid thoughts, feelings or conversations associated with the trauma (d) hyper-vigilance and (e) psychological numbing.

Mr. ████ ████ reported having recurring distressing recollections or flashbacks of past trauma events. He stated, "I have flashbacks constantly about the incident. I think about it like 4 times per week." Mr. ████ ████ reported having intense psychological distress and physiological reactivity at exposure to triggers. He stated, "Every single day, I get triggered when I look at my baby girl because I think about what could have happened if I lost my wife or child that day. We were close to death and I am grateful that they didn't take our lives." Mr. ████ ████ reported making an effort to avoid thoughts, feelings or conversations associated with the trauma. He stated, "I have a hard time talking about this. I hate being asked about it because remembering this is like I am re-living it." Mr. ████ ████ reported being hyper-vigilant. He stated, "I am very hyper-vigilant wherever I go because I fear it happening again." Mr. ████ ████ reported experiencing psychological numbing when faced with situations that arouse recollections of the trauma. He stated, "I try to feel numb about it because I want to leave it in the past as opposed to re-living it over and over again."

Mr. ████ ████ reported experiencing trauma symptoms for the past 6 months, on an intermittent basis, as a result of the assault and trauma he experienced. Mr. ████ ████ symptoms hinder his ability to function with normal daily activities, such as trying to perform simple daily tasks. The intensity of his symptoms leads to thoughts of a sense of a foreshortened future, such as not expecting to have a healthy or normal lifestyle.

TREATMENT PLAN

Mr. ████ ████ treatment plan consists of various interventions aimed at helping him manage his trauma symptoms. Self-relaxation techniques and cognitive skills have been introduced to help Mr. ████ ████ cope with his trauma symptoms. It is recommended that Mr. ████ ████ receive outpatient mental health services on a monthly or as needed basis.

DIAGNOSTIC FORMULATION

The *Diagnostic and Statistical Manual of Mental Disorders* (*DSM*) is the standard classification of mental disorders used by mental health professionals in the United States. It is intended to be applicable in a wide array of contexts and used by clinicians and researchers of many different orientations (e.g., biological, psychodynamic, cognitive, behavioral, interpersonal). The *Diagnostic and Statistical Manual of Mental Disorders, Fifth Edition* (*DSM-5*) is the current edition and has been designed for use across clinical settings (inpatient, outpatient, partial hospital, consultation-liaison, clinic, private practice, and primary care), with community populations. In accordance with the DSM-5 diagnostic criteria, Mr. ████ ████ diagnostic classifications are listed as follows:

F33.2 **Major Depressive Disorder, Recurrent, Severe Without Psychotic Features**
F41.1 **Generalized Anxiety Disorder**
F43.10 **Post Traumatic Stress Disorder (PTSD)**

CONCLUSIONS

During my evaluation of Mr. ████ ████ the fear that he experienced, as he was assaulted and robbed, was repeatedly articulated as the main source of his psychological symptoms. Based on his trauma experience and my clinical assessment, I have concluded that Mr. ████ ████ symptoms were triggered as a result of the above-mentioned incident.

If you should have any questions concerning this case, or in need of further clarification, please contact me at my office.

Sincerely,

Adriana Reyes, RAMFT (97937)	Celina Marciano, LMFT, PsyD (MFC 42997)
Registered Associate MFT	Licensed Marriage and Family Therapist
	Doctor of Psychology

Exhibit '19'

Declaration of Applicant about Physical and Mental Assault of the Criminal activity perpetuated against the Family

I, declare the following:

1. I have personal knowledge of all the facts contained in this declaration, and if called upon to testify I would do so.

2. I was born in Guadalajara, Jalisco, Mexico on November 20, 1989. My first entry into the United States was in July of 2004. I entered the United States by means of a car with a family I knew. I left the United States on January 3, 2011 because I had an immigration hold in San Francisco so I decided to sign a voluntary deportation document and leave the United States. I then tried to come back into the United States on July 16, 2011 with a fraudulent green card but I was caught at the border and returned to Mexico. I then tried to enter the United States the following week in July of 2011 by means of a car. I have been in the United States since my last entry in July of 2011. I have been residing in the United States for 7 years now. I am married to . We have 3 United States citizen children: 8-year-old , 5-year-old , and 1-year-old . I reside with my wife and children.

3. On January 27, 2018, approximately 3:00 p.m., my family and I went to visit my cousin and her family in Oakland, CA. We had spent the whole day there while all the children were playing. We had let our sons sleep over at my cousin's house. We had left the house around 10:15 p.m. when we realized that we had left our baby bottle at the house. We drove back to the house on Bancroft avenue when we noticed a honda accord parked there. As we were walking toward the house on the 2100 block of 102nd avenue approximately at 10:15 p.m. when we were approached by two males we did not know. One of the males pulled out a firearm and hit my wife, l, in the mouth with his fists while she was holding our young daughter, in her arms.The same male demanded her possessions. My wife was too afraid to react so she gave this male her purse, debit card, and Iphone.

4. The incident happened so quickly. I didn't have enough time to respond and protect my wife and child because the second male approached me and started to kick and punch me several times demanding my belongings. Since they had firearms pointed at us, and was afraid that either I, my wife, or my daughter may have gotten shot, I gave this second male my Iphone and I watch. After they had beaten and robbed us, the two males then fled eastbound on Bancroft Avenue.

5. All together, these two males who committed this crime took my wife's purse, debit card, two cellular phones, one apple Iwatch. I estimate that we were robbed of at least $1600 worth of items. I had immediately called the police and they arrived immediately. Upon arrival, the Police Officer noticed that my wife had blood on her lip and somehow my daughter also had a blood on her lip. I had swelling on the right side of my face. My wife and I told the Police Officer that we had just been attacked and robbed. The Police Officer had medical personnel come to our location and help us with the injuries we had sustained during the attack.We were transported to Eden Hospital by PMP 2222 for further assessment (Please see **Exhibits 3 and 4**). The criminal investigation report was filed under Report number 18-004869 (Please see **Exhibit 3**).

6. We had told the Police Officers everything that had happened including all the details of what we could remember as the incident happened so fast. We had also offered our cooperation to the Oakland Police Department should they need to ask us any more questions. On February 5, 2018, Lieutenant Robert ROSIN, the Commander of the Robbery/Burglary division of the Oakland

Police Department (Please see **Exhibit** 5) had written my wife a letter stating that they were doing everything they could to apprehend the perpetrators of this crime but unless we could provide more detailed information, the crime didn't warrant any further investigation. But Lt. ROSIN had also stated that should we remember anything else, we could call him with any other information we had remembered.

7. The two persons who committed this crime have not been apprehended yet. The suspects were never apprehended and I worry because I do not know what is going to happen to me or my family once they are found. I do not know what will happen if they are apprehended, serve their time, and then are released. They would blame me for their hardship and I do not know what they would either do to me or my family.

8. This incident had a lasting and permanent effect on my life. I have become more anxious than I used to be and I am always worried about who is around me or my family. Since that day, I have had a lot of trouble sleeping. I have seen Dr. ████, a Psychologist who is helping me deal with this situation (Please see **Exhibit 2**) to see if I can get some help with my constant anxiety and fear. I have a lot of trouble sleeping as well. I was given medication to help me with these issues (Please see **Exhibit 4**). I had thought that over time, I would start to get better but I am not. Not while the two persons who committed this crime have not been apprehended yet.

9. I even have to keep my dog inside the house because if I let him out, I am afraid that something bad will happen to him. I also lock my garage door and keep all my doors locked now whether it is in the garage or inside the house. I can't even sleep normally like I used to before this criminal act happened. I know for a fact that I have lost confidence in myself. When I go somewhere, I always come back to the house at least 3 times to check if I locked everything. I was never like this before. When I walk anywhere, I am always looking behind me or near me to see who is around. I feel very paranoid now. I don't like living this. Even though the criminal act happened 6 months ago, I am still afraid because I know the persons who committed this crime have not been apprehended.

10. I have been diagnosed with 3 different conditions: 1) Major Depressive Disorder, Recurrent and Severe without Psychotic Features, 2) Generalized Anxiety Disorder, and 3) Post Traumatic Stress Disorder (PTSD) due to the frequency, intensity, and duration of my symptoms (Please see **Exhibit 2**). My symptoms only began when this criminal act was perpetrated against my family and I. My response to the event involved intense fear, helplessness and terror.

11. The symptoms I have been experiencing from Major Depressive Disorder alone involve sadness and depressed mood, crying spells, irritability, feelings of guilt, loss of interest, energy and motivation, decrease of sleep, and nightmares with morbid themes (despair-Please see **Exhibit 2**). Before the event, I had not experienced any of these symptoms. Even after 6 months since the event, I can't get back to the way I was. I used to have a positive attitude about life, even when I was going through a difficult time. I used to take control of problems and always moved forward. I just can't get that confidence back that I had before this event. I also cry, but only when I am alone, because I don't want to scare my wife or my children. All I want is to be a good father and I want the best for my wife and children.

12. I also get very irritated with myself because I used to let my children have more freedom than I do now. I feel like I am controlling their every move. I even feel guilty by doing this but I need to

protect them and make sure they are safe. I used to have more energy so I could do more things with my children like take them to the park, take them out to eat, or go on vacations with them but now, because of my loss of energy and interest, I don't do those things anymore. I have to keep my children in the house more now so I can make sure they are safe. I used to take my wife out on dates as well but I can't even do that anymore because I have to make sure that she is safe. I am so afraid that this criminal act will happen again. I have been living in this fear for the last 6 months. My lack of sleep is due to the fear that this criminal action will happen again to my family and I. My nightmares involve people following me and I am unable to run. I try to protect my wife and children but I can't. I don't know how much longer I can live with this paranoia, fear, and anxiety.

13. Over the last 6 months, the symptoms have been up and down but mostly they have been progressively increasing. I think it is because of the unsurety of my immigration issues. I am trying to become an U.S. Citizen but I am afraid that I will be taken away from from my family. That is my ultimate fear. I can not live without my family and they can't live without me. I pray that one day my immigration issues are resolved so I can move on and take better care of my family by being a better father and husband even though I am doing the best I can.

14. I have also been experiencing symptoms consistent with Generalized Anxiety Disorder such as excessive anxiety and worry, nervousness, restlessness, difficulty with concentration, headaches, and panic attacks (Please see **Exhibit 2**). As stated previously, I am anxious and nervous constantly because I am afraid that this will happen again. I even bite my nails which I never have done before. I feel restless and am always moving around. I am always looking around and fidgeting no matter where I am. I can't focus or concentrate. I have headaches often because of the stress that my body carries.

15. I also have panic attacks since the incident happened where I can't breathe and my body feels hot. When I think about what happened and that it might happen again, the panic attack begins. I didn't even know what a panic attack was until this incident happened. These symptoms also hinder my ability to function with normal daily activities, such as trying to perform simple daily tasks. The intensity of my symptoms lead to thoughts of a foreshortened future, such as not expecting to have a healthy and normal lifestyle which is also affecting not just me, but my wife and children.

16. Lastly, my symptoms have been consistent with Post Traumatic Stress Disorder such as recurring distressing collections or flashbacks of prior trauma events, intense psychological distress at exposure to triggers, efforts to avoid thoughts, feelings or conversations associated with the trauma, hypervigilance, and psychological numbing (Please see **Exhibit 2**). I have had constant flashbacks about what happened on that day. It makes me go back to that day every day when I look at my baby girl or my wife and think of what could have happened to them and the unsurety of what I would do if I lost either one of them. We were close to death on that day, and at least I am thankful for the fact that they didn't take our lives. I hate being asked about it, even after all these years, because it brings me back to the incident and it is like I am reliving it all over again and again. What I really want is to stop reliving the incident in my mind and move on in my life.

17. I can be treated for these conditions in the United States. I would not be able to receive the same medical treatment in Mexico as I do in the United States. If I am returned to Mexico, I will have very limited access to healthcare. My family would not continue to reside in the United States if I have to go back to Mexico. My wife and 3 children would have to relocate with me. There would

is very poor. Unlike the United States, Mexico does not have an efficient health financing scheme. In fact, Mexico's healthcare system is highly inadequate. The local Mexicans who can afford healthcare, seek medical help from abroad.

18. The top disease in Mexico is Hepatitis A which affects the entire country. According to **'The Borgen Project,'** The Blog, Top Diseases in Mexico, Symptoms, Prevalence & Treatment, October 2016:

> *"Hepatitis A can be spread via contaminated food or water or spread through person-to-person contact. A person to person transmission can occur when an infected person's stool is ingested by a non-infected person through poor hygiene Practices. Poor hygiene and sanitation practices are the results of letting half the country's population live in abject poverty; without clean drinking water or sewage services, Hepatitis A spreads easily and is now endemic to the population of Mexico. To clarify, if a disease is endemic that means the illness is regularly found among a population; for Mexico, Hepatitis A is found throughout the entire country."*

This is only one example. There are many other diseases that are prevalent in Mexico (Please see **Exhibit 19**). My family is relatively healthy right now and even if we did get sick, we could get immediate medical attention in the United States. If I am returned to Mexico, I would most likely end up with one of these diseases and so would my wife and children should we have to relocate to Mexico.

19. One of the biggest problems of Mexico is the Mexican drug war. The Mexican drug war is a killing machine and the level of violence and slaughter is similar to conventional warfare. Mexico is the center for illegal harvesting of opium and marijuana drugs. Drug cartels are the organized crime syndicates involved in the production, distribution and sale of drugs. The unemployed youth are forced to get into drug trades; so finding a job in Mexico will be very difficult. I am afraid, that with all the peer pressure my children would be under if they relocate to Mexico with me and grow into teenagers there, they would always have the possibility of ending up getting into drugs and criminal activity. In California, my children, at least, have the opportunities of being educated in the United States and they will have a very good chance of getting a job. I am scared that I might be pulled into the drug trades just to make enough money to survive and support my family. Drug violence is a big problem in Mexico and the casualties in the drug wars are very high.

20. Violence in Mexico is also a prevalent and widespread problem. If I am returned to Mexico, I am afraid that I would be the victim of another criminal act. I haven't even gotten over the criminal act that happened to me and my family 6 months ago. I almost have a panic attack every time I think about returning to Mexico and what might happen to me there. I am having a lot of trouble now trying to protect and make sure my family is safe in the United States. I can't even imagine trying to keep them safe in Mexico with the widespread crime and cartel activity. An article from Amnesty International states:

> *"Violence increased throughout Mexico. The armed forces continued to undertake regular policing functions. Human rights defenders and journalists were threatened, attacked and killed; digital attacks and surveillance were particularly common. Widespread arbitrary detentions continued to lead to torture and other ill-treatment, enforced disappearances and extrajudicial*

executions. Impunity persisted for human rights violations and crimes under international law. Mexico received a record number of asylum claims, mostly From nationals of El Salvador, Honduras, Guatemala and Venezuela. Violence against women remained a major concern; new data showed that two thirds of women had experienced gender-based violence during their lives. The rights to housing and education were compromised by two major earthquakes" (Please see ***Exhibit 15****).*

Another section from the same article states:

> *"There was a marked increase in the number of homicides, with 42,583 recorded nationally, the highest annual number of homicides registered by authorities since the start of the presidential term in December 2012. The real number may be higher, with some crimes not being reported to police, and not all of those reported triggering official action." (Please see* ***Exhibit 15****).*

21. The economy in Mexico is very poor and it will be very difficult to live in Mexico knowing how the situation is. There are numerous problems in Mexico like high crime rates, drugs, corruption and a troubled economy. Mexico is considered to be a very highly undesirable country to live in due to its appalling social, economic and political conditions. In the condition I am in now, I know I would not be able to handle living in Mexico knowing how bad the economy and the criminal activity is.

22. Poverty has been a persistent problem in Mexico. At least half the Mexican population lives in poverty making Mexico rank behind Kazakhstan, Bulgaria and Thailand. Lack of and unavailability of education and unemployment are the major reasons for poverty in Mexico. Life without a stable and well-paying job in Mexico will be extremely difficult for me. I couldn't live with myself knowing that I am not providing the best I can for my family. In Mexico, I couldn't even support myself, let alone my whole family.

23. I am so afraid of what would happen to my wife and daughter if we had to relocate to Mexico. Fortunately, I have a chance of protecting them while living in the United States. Widespread violence against women and girls is widespread in Mexico. Once again, quoting from Amnesty International,

> *"Gender-based violence against women and girls was widespread. Most of the cases were inadequately investigated and perpetrators enjoyed impunity. Sufficient and current data on gender-based killings was not available. However, official data for 2016 was published indicating that 2,668 women were considered to be victims of homicide, pending further investigations. In August, the National Institute of Statistics and Geography published a survey estimating that 66.1% of Girls and women aged 15 or above had experienced gender-based violence at least once in their lives, and that 43.5% of women had experienced gender-based violence committed by their partners."*

24. For the reasons stated above, I believe the only way to keep this family going and to maintain a healthy and stable life is if I am allowed to stay in the United States. My family means everything to me. Without my wife and children, I would fall apart.

ABOUT THE AUTHOR

Brian D. Lerner is an Immigration Lawyer and runs a National Immigration Law Firm for nearly 30 years. He is an attorney who is a certified specialist that might help in Immigration & Nationality Law as issued by the California State Bar, Board of Legal Specialization. Attorney Lerner is an expert in Immigration Law, Removal and Deportation, Citizenship, Waiver and Appeals.

He has been a licensed attorney since 1992 and started the Law Offices of Brian D. Lerner, APC. The immigration practice consists of Immigration and Nationality Law, and everything involved with and regarding immigration which includes citizenship, investment visas, family and employment visas, removal and deportation hearings, appeals, waivers, adjustment, consulate processing and all types of immigration and citizenship matters.

He has represented clients from all over the U.S. and in many countries around the world. One side of his practice is dedicated to keeping people in the U.S. and fighting for their immigration rights, while another side is to get people back who have been deported and removed from the U.S.

Also, there is the affirmative part of Immigration Law which Brian Lerner has helped numerous people come into the U.S. on business visas, investment visas, student visas, fiancée and marriage visas, religious visas and many more. Attorney Lerner has helped immigrants who are victims of crime and domestic violence or ones that are married to abusers.

In other words, Attorney Lerner has a firm that helps people all over the U.S. He has dedicated significant time to preparing numerous petitions and applications for you to get at a fraction of the price of hiring an attorney. He says it is the next best thing to a real attorney because they are real petitions prepared by an expert.

www.ingramcontent.com/pod-product-compliance
Lightning Source LLC
Chambersburg PA
CBHW061355240926
51846CB00007B/1416